THE YOUNG ROMANTICS

The Young Romantics
Paris 1827-37

LINDA KELLY

THE BODLEY HEAD
LONDON   SYDNEY
TORONTO

To My Parents

CONTENTS

Authors Note, vii

[1] 1827, *1*

[2] 1828, *14*

[3] 1829, *24*

[4] 1830, *36*

[5] 1831, *50*

[6] 1832, *62*

[7] 1833, *75*

[8] 1834, *89*

[9] 1835, *100*

[10] 1836, *112*

[11] 1837, *123*

Appendix : Translations, 133

Bibliography, 139

Index, 143

ILLUSTRATIONS
(following page 84)

Victor Hugo in 1829. From a lithograph by Achille Devéria.
(*Lalance/Ziolo*)

Charles Nodier's salon at the Arsenal, 1831. From an engraving
by Tony Johannot. (*Lalance/Ziolo*)

Charles Augustin Sainte-Beuve in 1831. From an engraving
by Demary. (*Lalance/Ziolo*)

Adèle Hugo c. 1832. From a painting by Louis Boulanger.
(*The Mansell Collection*)

Léopoldine Hugo drawn by her mother, April 1837.
(*Lalance/Ziolo*)

11 Rue Notre-Dame-des-Champs, Victor Hugo's home
from 1827 to 1830. (*Lalance/Ziolo*)

Alfred de Vigny in 1831. From a lithograph by Achille Devéria.
(*The Mansell Collection*)

Alexandre Dumas in 1829. From a lithograph by Achille Devéria.
(*The Mansell Collection*)

'Ballade à la Lune': self-portrait by Alfred de Musset, 1834.
(*Bulloz*)

'Ode à la Colonne': frontispiece by Cousin for the 1828 edition
of Victor Hugo's *Odes et Ballades*. (*Lalance/Ziolo*)

'Les Romantiques': a contemporary view of the romantics
of the 1830's. (*Jean-Loup Charmet/Ziolo*)

Hernani: The final scene. From a lithograph
by Eugène Devéria. (*Lalance/Ziolo*)

Erection of a barricade, July 29, 1830. From a lithograph
by Bellangé. (*Jean-Loup Charmet/Ziolo*)

ILLUSTRATIONS

Juliette Drouet in 1832. From a lithograph by Léon Noël.
(*Radio Times Hulton Picture Library*)

Mademoiselle George. From a painting by Gérard.
(*Radio Times Hulton Picture Library*)

Charles Nodier. From a lithograph by Emile Lasalle.
(*Radio Times Hulton Picture Library*)

Mademoiselle Mars. From a lithograph by Achille Devéria.
(*Lalance/Ziolo*)

Alfred de Musset in 1831. Bronze medallion
by David d'Angers. (*Lalance/Ziolo*)

George Sand drawn by Alfred de Musset, 1833.
(*Jean-Loup Charmet/Ziolo*)

Marie Dorval in the role of Marion de Lorme, 1831.
From a lithograph by Achille Devéria. (*Lalance/Ziolo*)

Author's Note

I have always loved the plays and poetry of the French romantics but
it was not until, in the course of writing a book on the poet Chatterton,
I read about Alfred de Vigny's *Chatterton* and its impact on the Parisian
audiences of 1835 that I began to be fascinated by their world as well.
To read about Alfred de Vigny was to read about his great contemporaries, for their lives were so interwoven and literary Paris was so
small, that the study of one led to another.

When I had finished the book on Chatterton I returned to the world
of the French romantics and the letters, diaries and memoirs of the
period. An enormous amount has been written about the leading figures
of the French romantic movement, their letters have been meticulously
edited, and their own literary output was immense. Amidst such a
wealth of material my chief interest has been to unravel their changing
relationships with one another during the years when the romantic
revolution, which they helped to bring about, was at its height. I have
been led on, above all, by the fascination of their personalities and the
charm which, over the space of nearly one hundred and fifty years,
they continue to exert.

One of the pleasures of writing this book has been my return to the
poetry of the romantic period, but I have been much exercised as to
whether or not to include translations. On the one hand I feel that
serious poetry should not be mangled, on the other, since the poetry in
almost every case is directly relevant to the narrative it could be irritating for a reader to miss the point of a quotation for lack of a vital word
or two. So I have provided translations in prose at the back, keeping
them as literal as sense and grammar will allow. I hope that those who
have recourse to them will linger there as short a time as possible.

I would like to thank Jonathan Cape, the Estate of André Maurois
and the Estate of Babette Johanna Hopkins for permission to use
Gerard Hopkins' translation of the passage from *Elle et Lui* on p. 87
from his translation of André Maurois' *Lélia: La Vie de George Sand.*

L.K.

THE YOUNG ROMANTICS

1827

One morning, early in January 1827, a slight red-haired young man rang the bell of a small apartment above a joiner's shop in the Rue de Vaugirard. His name was Charles-Augustin Sainte-Beuve. He was twenty-two, the only son of a widowed mother, a medical student who in the intervals of his studies had already begun a promising career as a literary critic. He was calling on Victor Hugo, a young poet whom he had never met but whose latest volume of poems he had just reviewed in the liberal paper the *Globe*.

The *Globe*, an influential, somewhat academic journal, had hitherto shown little sympathy for Hugo and his fellow poets of the romantic school. The romantics, for the most part, were royalist and Catholic, the *Globe* was free-thinking and anti-clerical. Nor did their literary opinions agree. The *Globe*'s political convictions were in the traditions of the enlightened eighteenth century, and so too was its liking for classical proportion in the arts. The romantics, legitimist in politics, were considered revolutionary in literary matters. Hugo's gothic novel *Han d'Islande*, whose monstrous hero drank blood from human skulls, had shown romanticism at its most frenetic. 'If genius is close to madness,' wrote a critic, 'then the author of *Han d'Islande* may be said to approach genius.'

But Hugo's recently published *Odes et Ballades* could not be so easily dismissed. Here, whatever his previous reservations, the editor of the *Globe* could recognise a new voice in French poetry, a complement in literary terms to the *Globe*'s own desire for social and political renewal. He had handed the poems to Sainte-Beuve, a former pupil and his protégé on the paper. 'They're by that young barbarian Victor Hugo,' he told him, 'who has talent.'

Sainte-Beuve's review, the most important he had yet undertaken, gave an enthusiastic appreciation of Hugo's work since his first emergence, five years earlier, as a leader of the romantic school. Sainte-Beuve paid tribute to the grace and virtuosity of the new volume, Hugo's 'style of fire, glittering with images, leaping with harmonies', tempering his praises only with a warning against imaginative excess. 'In poetry, as elsewhere, nothing is more dangerous than too much force.'

Hugo, surprised and pleased by the review, coming as it did from a previously unfriendly quarter, had written to the editor to ask the address of his reviewer. Sainte-Beuve turned out to be a neighbour. Hugo lived at 90 Rue de Vaugirard, Sainte-Beuve at 94. Here the day before Hugo had called to express his thanks and, finding him out, had left his card. Sainte-Beuve was now returning his call.

The Hugos were at lunch when Sainte-Beuve was shown in. Madame Hugo, a dark-eyed, Spanish-looking beauty, was still in a morning négligé. Hugo rose to greet him. He was a pale young man with piercing hazel eyes, clean-shaven, soberly dressed, not tall but with an immediate presence. He had a grave and candid face, a long finely chiselled nose, brown hair brushed back from a broad and lofty forehead—its monumental proportions the delight of caricaturists in later years. The mark of power was on that brow. Hugo was twenty-four, triumphantly happy in his marriage, conscious of genius and a growing fame. Sainte-Beuve, echoing his editor, described the Hugo of this period as a 'young barbarian king'.

At first sight the contrast between the two young men seemed painful. Sainte-Beuve too was short, but frail and ill-proportioned, with a round head too large for his body. An intimate disability, a malformation of the urethra, intensified his sense of physical inferiority and his natural diffidence with women. 'O cruel nature,' wrote a contemporary, 'to give a poet the sense of beauty and a thirst for love and to hide his soul behind a comic mask.'

But a brilliant intelligence lit up and redeemed Sainte-Beuve's unattractive countenance; his expression, unless he was crossed, was tolerant and good-humoured. His conversation was halting, with sentences left unfinished as though in despair at the complexity of things, but subtle, witty and insinuating. Young though he was, and still not committed to a literary career, he had already shown himself to be a critic of exceptional ability, his judgement backed by enormous erudition, the acuteness of his insights, he later maintained, owing something to his scientific training. The dissection of souls, of moods, of ideas, was Sainte-Beuve's true forte.

Today, meeting Hugo, he was nervous and confused at first, his confusion increased by the presence of Madame Hugo from whom, with an instinct resembling prudery, he kept his eyes averted. She in her turn paid little attention to him, lapsing before long into an abstracted silence from which, when Sainte-Beuve got up to go, her husband had to rouse her. A young mother, recently recovered from the birth of her third child, and still breast-feeding a baby son, she had other preoccupations than poetry.

For it was poetry, after Hugo's first thanks and compliments, that was the subject of their conversation. Sainte-Beuve had written poetry

[2]

himself but had shown it to no one. New worlds opened out as he listened to Hugo. Hugo spoke of the art of poetry, the secrets of rhythm and colour, the techniques and 'fingerings' of the new poetic method. Sainte-Beuve, who had recently embarked on a study of the French poets of the sixteenth century, like the romantics innovators in form and metre, responded eagerly, finding new, and hitherto unsuspected parallels, between the Pléiade and the romantic school. Till then, liberal and rationalist, temperamentally repelled by the royalism and mysticism of the romantics, Sainte-Beuve had not sought contact with them. Now, swept along by Hugo's 'vast discourse', his reservations, for the time being, disappeared. 'From that day,' he wrote, 'began my initiation into the romantic school of poetry.'

The first meeting was soon followed by others, Hugo being quick to recognise Sainte-Beuve's value as a critic, scholar and ally in the liberal press, Sainte-Beuve expanding in the glow of Hugo's personality, his medical studies neglected, the stringencies of the *Globe* forgotten as he moved towards the 'enchanted isle of poetry'. Older friends looked on sceptically. 'You will grow out of it,' said one; 'you are like a young man in love.'

Sainte-Beuve took little notice. Diffidently he sent his poems, the poems he had shown to no one, to Hugo. 'Come quickly, my friend,' wrote Hugo in reply, 'so that I can thank you for the fine verses you have entrusted to me. I'd like to tell you too that I had already guessed, less by your articles, remarkable though they are, than by your looks and conversation, that you were a poet. Let me then be a little proud of my perspicacity, let me congratulate myself on having sensed the presence of so great a talent.'

Years later, when friendship between the two had turned to bitter enmity, Sainte-Beuve could still remember the generosity of Hugo's first response and the delicacy with which, combining praise with criticism, he had shown him where his weaknesses lay. 'When I read Hugo's *Odes et Ballades*,' he said at a dinner at Magny's, 'I took my poems to him . . . The people on the *Globe* called him a barbarian. All the same, everything that I have done *he* made me do.'

*　　*　　*

In the spring of 1827 the Hugos moved house. The little flat above the joiner's shop had been too cramped for entertaining, Hugo's ambitions and his income were increasing. They found a new apartment in the Rue Notre-Dame-des-Champs not far away, a quiet tree-lined street, still unpaved, and only a short walk from the open fields. Sainte-Beuve, whether by accident or design, had moved to the same street a few weeks before. Lamartine, visiting him there, was charmed by the peace and seclusion of his new home: 'your mother, the garden, the doves, the peace . . . which remind me of those gentle priests and country presbyteries I used to love in my childhood.'

No such peace reigned in Hugo's apartment, which was lively with childrens' voices and with streams of visitors, though a spacious garden behind the house with poplars and an ornamental pond spanned by a rustic bridge gave the illusion of a country setting. Inside he had rented the whole first floor: two bedrooms, a dining-room, a study and, most important, a large and handsome drawing-room, its walls hung with prints and paintings of the romantic school and, in the place of honour, the golden lily of the *Jeux Floraux* at the Academy of Toulouse, the poetry prize awarded to Hugo in his eighteenth year. Here, in the 'chambre au lys d'or', as it was called, Hugo for the first time had space to receive the growing number of his friends and followers and to found a salon and a school. Sainte-Beuve, before long its most assiduous member, would christen the group the Cénacle— the word, deriving from the *Cène* or Last Supper, is used to describe a fervent literary or artistic confraternity.

In this case it was both. Hugo, who rivalled his artistic contemporaries in painting, was passionately interested in art and architecture. His own poems, well thumbed and splashed with paint, lay side by side with the works of Byron, Goethe and Walter Scott in the studios of Paris. 'Fraternité des arts', wrote Sainte-Beuve, in his poem 'Le Cénade'.

Round Hugo, over the next few years, would gather almost every star, risen and rising, in the romantic firmament. Not since the Renaissance, as the romantics themselves pointed out, had such a constellation lit the literary and artistic heavens. Here came Lamartine, an occasional and honoured visitor; Alfred de Vigny, blonde and aristocratic, who shared with Hugo and Lamartine the triple crown of romantic poetry; Emile Deschamps, poet, dandy, lover of Spain and Shakespeare, and his brother Antony; Balzac, still little known; Prosper Mérimée; the ebullient Alexandre Dumas; Gérard de Nerval; Théophile Gautier; Alfred de Musset. Here too came Delacroix, his polished manners belying his revolutionary reputation as a painter, and with him other artists of the romantic school: Tony Johannot, the illustrator, whose charming vignettes decorated the poems and novels of the romantics; the sculptor David d'Angers; Eugène and Achille Devéria; Louis Boulanger, one of Hugo's closest friends, 'an intelligence' he considered, 'open to Shakespeare and Rembrandt alike'. Musical figures were less common. Hugo had no great feeling for music though Liszt, the prodigy of the Paris salons, would play in his apartment and Berlioz was an admirer and later an acquaintance. Few of the guests had reached their thirtieth year, some, like Musset, were still in their teens. 'It will be remarked,' wrote Dumas in his memoirs, 'that these great revolutionaries were very young.'

The Hugos' hospitality was very simple. Hugo, after early struggles with poverty, kept a close eye on the household accounts. Once Mérimée, a gifted cook, donned an apron to make *macaroni à l'italienne*, a success, wrote Madame Hugo, that equalled that of his books. More often cups of weak tea were the only refreshment served. 'You had to be all soul when you went there,' said a visitor, 'and leave your stomach in the hall.'

But Hugo, young, brilliant, breathing energy and gaiety, was a magnetic host, Madame Hugo an affable if sometimes absent-minded hostess. In looks at least she seemed the match of Victor, tall, opulently curved, with a regal carriage and magnificent dark eyes. She did not however shine in conversation, sometimes retreating into a 'mysterious apathy', her defence perhaps against the imperious personalities round her, at other times joining in with misplaced animation. 'Madame Hugo,' said an unkind guest, 'has all the pretensions of a wit, which is a pity.' Later Hugo would notice this and suffer before his friends, silencing her with a devastating glance. But in 1827 he was still deeply in love with his wife and devoted to their two small children,* Léopoldine and Charles, who would run among the guests or make for safety on his knee. The domestic happiness of the 'holy family' was one of the charms of the Rue Notre-Dame-des-Champs.

Hugo's salon was soon the chief romantic gathering place, but it was only one of many in the Paris of the period. In the Rue Abbaye-au-Bois Madame Récamier, still beautiful at fifty, held court. Every afternoon from three to five Chateaubriand, her lover of twenty years' standing, would arrive to take tea and the conversation would dance to his tune. Alfred de Vigny's salon was aristocratic as well as literary in flavour; he referred to the inhabitants of the Faubourg Saint-Germain as 'le grand monde'. Stendhal, witty and paradoxical, was the star of liberal salons. Over forty and too much of an individualist to join the Cénacle, he spoke of Hugo as 'le bonhomme Hugo', an affront to the poet's youthful dignity.

Best known of all, and until 1827 the centre of the romantic movement, was the salon of Charles Nodier, librarian of the Arsenal. Nodier was a bibliophile and scholar, a literary chameleon, classical in the purity of his style, romantic in his love of the fantastic. He had written fairy stories, poetry, gothic melodramas; he had compiled a dictionary; he was learned in botany and science; like Sainte-Beuve, who was

---

* Their first child, Léopold, died in infancy.

introduced to him by Hugo, he was deeply interested in the poets of the sixteenth century. He had come to the Arsenal, once the residence of Henri IV's great minister Sully, and now a royal library, in 1824, at the age of forty-four, after an erratic and impecunious life.

His Sunday evenings were famous. The white-panelled Renaissance salon with its crimson curtains and gilded mouldings made an elegant setting. Outside, the balcony looked over the river and the poplars of the island of Louvier, and in the summer the croaking of frogs was an accompaniment to the talk within. Madame Nodier, plump and bourgeoise, though at first over-awed by her surroundings, had soon domesticated them and an evening at the Arsenal had an almost family feeling —a feeling accentuated by the youth of her guests. Refreshments— little cakes and glasses of sugared water—were modest. The Nodiers, like most of their guests, were not rich, though an occasional visitor from the world of fashion brought a whiff of wealth and luxury with him.

From eight to ten the evening would be given up to talk of art and literature, its seriousness laced with flirtation. At the Nodiers' salon, more noticeably than at the Hugos', there was always a scattering of pretty girls. Nodier's lively daughter Marie, just out of the schoolroom, was one of the chief attractions, the subject later on of the famous sonnet of Arvers: 'Mon âme a son secret, ma vie a son mystère . . .'

On good evenings, Nodier, an incomparable story-teller, would take the floor with some reminiscence of his youth. Languid, witty, his willowy form draped against the fireplace, his face serenely melancholy, he seemed, wrote Dumas, like 'a mixture of Walter Scott and Perrault, the savant grappling with the poet, memory battling with imagination'. Newcomers would bow and creep to their places while the story lasted. It always seemed to end too soon. 'Enough of prose', he would finish, 'let us have poetry, poetry', and, sliding into his armchair by the fire, he would turn with a smile to one of the poets there—Hugo perhaps, or Vigny, more rarely Lamartine—who without moving from his place, shoulders propped against the wall, would launch on some poetic flight. Later Musset, aged barely nineteen, would read his first poems there.

At ten o'clock Marie Nodier would take to the piano, there would be dancing and games of cards; Nodier, a passionate but unlucky gambler, absorbed himself in écarté till the end of the evening. Hugo, deeply prudish, never danced. He considered the waltz lascivious and had once at a ball described the women in low-cut dresses as 'whited sepulchres'. He had been younger then but he still watched his wife with a jealous eye and would not permit his friends to address her by her christian name. As for other women, wrote an observer, he seemed all arms and legs in their presence.

[6]

'Gais comme l'oiseau sur la branche',

wrote Musset, recalling the charm of those evenings,

Le dimanche,
Nous rendions parfois matinal
L'Arsenal . . .

Quelqu'un récitait quelque chose,
Vers ou prose,
Puis nous courions recommencer
A danser . . .

Alors, dans la grande boutique
Romantique,
Chacun avait, maître ou garçon,
Sa chanson. . . .

Hugo portait déjà dans l'âme
Notre-Dame,
Et commençait à s'occuper
D'y grimper.

De Vigny chantait sur sa lyre
Ce beau sire
Qui mourut sans mettre à l'envers
Ses bas verts . . .

Sainte-Beuve faisait dans l'ombre
Douce et sombre,
Pour un oeil noir, un blanc bonnet,
Un sonnet.

Et moi de cet honneur insigne
Trop indigne,
Enfant par hasard adopté
Et gâté,

Je brochais des ballades, l'une
À la lune,
L'autre à deux yeux noirs et jaloux
Andaloux . . .*

By 1827 Nodier's position as host and patron of the romantic movement was beginning to slip. He noted with a certain wryness the

* For the translation of this, and subsequent verse quotations, see Appendix, p. 132.

growing ascendancy of Hugo. Hugo was preparing for battle, he saw literature in all-or-nothing terms. Nodier had wider sympathies, but you cannot win battles if you see everybody's point of view.

*   *   *

What was the battle? What were the aims of the romantics? Why was the subject the focus of such violent interest?

Hugo and his generation were all 'enfants du siècle', all, give or take a year or two, born with the century. Brought up amidst the dramas of Napoleon's wars, they had reached manhood to the anticlimax of peace and Bourbon rule. Restless and dissatisfied, their dreams of military glory frustrated, they had turned themselves instead towards the liberation of the arts, their foes no longer the armies of Europe but the tyrannies of classical tradition.

For thirty years, while the nation's energies had been absorbed in politics and war, the arts had virtually stood still in France, frozen, through lack of challenge, in the classical attitudes of the old régime. The violent emotions and experiences of the Napoleonic era had done much to render them meaningless. 'Since the campaign in Russia,' said a former officer to Stendhal, '*Iphigénie en Aulide* no longer seems such a good play.'

By the 1820s, while the academic establishment, hiding its own sterility behind the great names of the past, continued to denounce all change, the ice of classicism was beginning to crack. New influences were crowding in from abroad, Chateaubriand, the 'enchanter', had cast his spell on the rising generation, the poetry of Lamartine, Hugo and Vigny heralded the spring. An old society lay in ruins; the tremendous forces which had overturned it were sweeping at last through the realms of art and literature, their momentum all the greater for having been so long delayed.

Nor, despite the seeming stability of the Restoration, had the political impetus of earlier years been spent. In the aftermath of the Empire exhaustion had brought a temporary longing for repose. Now, to the excitement of creative ferment was added a hidden dimension: a growing under-current of political dissent, as yet unexpressed for fear of reprisal. The romantic rebellion, with its claims for freedom in the arts, cloaked the political revolution once more preparing in the shadows.

In the early days of the Restoration Louis XVIII, a Bourbon who had indeed learned something, had tried to steer the tricky course between revolution and reaction, between censorship and disorder, and had to some extent succeeded. His brother Charles X, who followed him in 1824, showed no such desire to heal the divisions in his country or to recognise the achievements of Napoleon and the Revolution.

[8]

Obstinately set on putting back the clock, he had had himself crowned with mediaeval ceremony, indemnified the émigrés, passed laws condemning sacrilege, and increased the privileges of the church and aristocracy.

The press, representing a vigorous and articulate bourgeoisie, a class grown rich since the Revolution, was naturally a threat to the régime, and from Charles' accession onwards censorship had become increasingly severe. Thus the *Globe*, liberal and anti-clerical, could not always express itself directly, although from the tone of its articles on non-political subjects the enlightened could glean a hidden meaning. Discussions of artistic and literary freedom in this atmosphere took on a more than academic interest.

Surprisingly, in the first years of the Restoration the poets of the romantic school, Hugo, Vigny and Lamartine among them, had tended to be royalist and Catholic. But their attitude owed more to literary sources—the chivalrous mediaevalism of Walter Scott, Chateaubriand's *Génie du Christianisme*—than to any deep conviction. 'I will be Chateaubriand or nothing', wrote Hugo in his diary at fifteen, and Chateaubriand, responding to his youthful admiration, was said to have called him 'l'Enfant sublime'.

The anomaly could not continue; the reactionary policies of Charles X had shaken the romantic faith in throne and altar. In February 1827 Victor Hugo, recipient of a royal pension, took the first step away from his former loyalties. At a reception at the Austrian Embassy the bearers of Napoleonic titles awarded for victories won in Austria were announced without those titles, a deliberate insult to the Napoleonic era and, in the eyes of many, to France herself. Hugo, son of a Napoleonic general, gave voice to the public indignation in his 'Ode à la Colonne', published in Paris a few days later and reprinted all over France:

> Non, Frères! non, Français de cet âge d'attente!
> Nous avons tous grandi sur le seuil de la tente.
> Condamnés à la paix, aiglons bannis des cieux,
> Sachons du moins, veillant aux gloires paternelles,
> Garder de tout affront, jalouses sentinelles,
> Les armures de nos aïeux!

Hugo, the royalist, defended the honour of Napoleon. Young liberals, whose admiration for Napoleon matched their hostility to the Bourbons, began to see him as their spokesman. The liberal press drew closer to him and by association to the romantic cause. Sainte-Beuve's links with the *Globe*, and Hugo's new-found friendship with him would do much to further this *rapprochement*. By 1830, the year of climax for romantics and liberals alike, Hugo, his earlier beliefs abandoned, could proclaim in his preface to *Hernani*: 'Romanticism, so often ill defined . . . is no more than liberalism in the arts.'

*   *   *

The first night of *Hernani*, in 1830, would be the culmination of the romantic fight for freedom. It was in the theatre that the decisive battles would take place and rightly so, for in no other branch of the arts was the weight of tradition heavier. The Théâtre Français was the holy of holies of French classicism, Racine and Corneille were its gods. Their sculptured heads, with heavy wigs, provoked the scorn of the young romantics: the periwig had become the symbol of everything that was sterile and static in French theatre. Classical history provided the themes for tragedy, the three unities, of action, time and place, were strictly observed, actors and actresses, trained in the grand declamatory manner, spoke their parts in balanced alexandrines. Everyday words were replaced by elaborate periphrasis: a dog, to give an example among thousands, was called, 'de la fidélité le respectable soutien'.

While classicism reigned at the Théâtre Français, however, vigorously defended by actors whose talents expressed themselves best in this form, the popular theatre of the boulevards was showing a very different type of entertainment. Here melodrama held sway; dastardly bandits, angelic village maidens, crude cloak and dagger plots brought cheers and hisses from the audience. The acting had seldom been above the level of the plots, but in 1827 two actors of genius, Frédérick Lemaître and Marie Dorval, had scored a triumphant success in the play *Trente Ans dans la Vie d'un Joueur*. For the first time melodrama, though still confined to the popular theatre, could be judged on the level of art.

By 1827 too, the financial situation of the Théâtre Français was no longer impregnable. Their greatest actor, Talma, had died and with his death receipts from the box office had dropped. Theatrical controversy, such as the romantics promised to provide, might be one way to bring back the crowds.

Talma had been the glory of the classical theatre, but he himself had felt the limitations of the genre. In 1826, not long before his death, he had sat at dinner next to Victor Hugo and had spoken to him of his desire for more reality in the theatre, for a role which was human rather than heroic.

'The actor is nothing without his role,' he said, 'and I have never had a true one . . . You, Monsieur Hugo, you are young and bold, you should write me a part. I hear that you are writing a play about Cromwell. I have always wanted to play Cromwell . . . Tell me something about your play.'

'The part you dream of playing,' said Hugo, 'is the part I dream of writing,' and he began to expound his views on the theatre: the mingling of genres, the substitution of drama for classical tragedy, the suppression of rhetoric and fine verses.

'Ah yes,' cried Talma, 'above all no fine verses.' And at the end of the evening he seized Hugo's hand:

'Be quick and finish your play. I'm in a hurry to act in it.'

But Talma died soon after, and, lacking an actor of his stature for the leading part, Hugo had been in no hurry to finish *Cromwell*, expanding it instead to huge and unstageable proportions and crowding it with characters. It would remain a theoretical exposition of his views, reflecting in its choice of a republican hero a further shift from his earlier royalism. Behind the figure of Cromwell lay the vaster shadow of Napoleon, from now on to loom ever larger in Hugo's imagination.

*   *   *

The great theatrical event of 1827 was the arrival in Paris that autumn of a troupe of English players and the ensuing revelation of Shakespeare to French audiences. Four years before, Stendhal in his *Racine et Shakespeare* had compared the two in an essay that set out many of the aims of romantic drama. But at the time he wrote it French chauvinism, the wounds of Waterloo still smarting, was at its height. In 1822 a visiting troupe of players from England had been pelted with eggs and vegetables and hissed from the stage. 'Down with Shakespeare,' was the cry, 'he is a lieutenant of Wellington.'

In 1827 the public could afford to be more open-minded. The success in England of Mademoiselle George, the leading lady of French tragedy and moreover a former mistress of Napoleon, had opened the way for a return visit by an English company. The Odéon, Paris's second 'official' theatre, which shared with the Théâtre Français the monopoly of classical drama, was placed at their disposal and on a hot night in September, to a packed and curious audience, their first performance, *Hamlet*, was given with Charles Kemble and the young Irish actress Harriet Smithson in the leading roles.

'Universal stupefaction!' wrote Delacroix to Hugo. 'Hamlet raises his hideous head, Othello prepares his murderous pillow, subverting all dramatic law and order. Who knows what next? King Lear is about to tear out his eyes before French audiences. The dignity of the Academy demands that all imports of this kind should be declared incompatible with public morality. Farewell good taste! Whatever happens put on a stout cuirass beneath your clothes. Beware the daggers of the classicists.'

Both Delacroix and Hugo were in the audience that night and so were other young romantics, Vigny, Sainte-Beuve, Gérard de Nerval and Berlioz among them. Few of them could understand English. They perceived *Hamlet* through the mists of translation, taking their French cribs with them to the theatre. But the impression they received was overwhelming. The picturesque costumes, the freedom of construction, the mingling of tragedy and comedy, of violence and lyricism, the death scenes in public instead of discreetly off stage, the naturalism and freedom of the acting, so different from the 'Greek correctitude' of the classical theatre, were entirely new. No doubt the vehemence of the actors' gestures owed something to the fact that they were playing before a foreign audience but Kemble with his bitter laugh, seeming to reveal a whole philosophy of sardonic disillusion, was an unforgettable Hamlet, and Harriet Smithson—especially successful in the mad scene —was a heart-rending Ophelia.

A few days later came *Romeo and Juliet*. 'Ah, what a change from the leaden clouds and icy winds of Denmark to the burning sun, the perfumed nights of Italy!' wrote Berlioz. 'What a transition from the melancholy, the heartbreak, the cruel irony, the madness, the tears, the mourning, the lowering destiny of Hamlet to the ardent and impetuous love, immense, irresistible, pure and lovely as the smile of angels, the vengeance, the lost despairing kisses, the fatal conflict of love and death on the part of these hapless lovers! By the end of the third act, scarcely able to breathe, my heart as if gripped by an iron hand, I cried to myself, "I am lost, I am lost".'

The young composer fell hopelessly in love. Unable to work, he wandered aimlessly through Paris and the surrounding countryside, dreaming of Shakespeare and his Juliet, passing days without sleep, collapsing only from exhaustion, once among the corn stooks of a harvest field, once at a table at the Café du Cardinal, where he slept for five hours, to the great alarm of the waiters who thought he was dead and dared not go near him.

He had never met Miss Smithson. She had Paris at her feet. In England, where the grand manner of Mrs Siddons was the ideal, her gentle voice and soft Irish accent had been a disadvantage. Now she seemed dazed by the magnitude of her success. Night after night the streets were blocked by carriages outside the theatre; every section of the press, even the classicists, paid tribute to her beauty and her art. When Mademoiselle Mars, the queen of the Théâtre Français, took a box at the theatre, it seemed that her triumph was complete. 'Our actresses go to school,' wrote Delacroix, 'and stare their eyes out.'

'An English critic has stated in the *Illustrated London News*', wrote Berlioz in his memoirs, 'that on seeing Miss Smithson that night I said, "I shall marry Juliet and write my greatest symphony on the play". I did both,* but I never said anything of the kind . . . I was much too overwhelmed to entertain such dreams.'

While Berlioz paced the streets in a lover's frenzy, Victor Hugo returned home from the theatre and that very night, it is said, sat down to begin his preface to *Cromwell*. The play was completed and awaiting publication; the preface, imbued with his enthusiasm for the new 'god of the theatre', was published with it in December. It was Hugo's manifesto and would be that of the romantic movement. Sounding the battle-cry of 'nature and truth' in the arts, he proclaimed the ideal of drama in the Shakespearean manner—freedom from classical unities and conventions, the mingling of tragedy and comedy, the grotesque and the sublime, obedience to no rules save those of the poet's own inspiration. 'Let us take the hammer to theories, poetics and systems,' he wrote, 'let us fling down this ancient plasterwork which masks the face of art.'

Hugo's call resounded through every branch of the arts. While the classicists denounced him, the romantics rallied to him as their leader. 'To the younger generation,' wrote Théophile Gautier in his *Histoire du Romantisme*, 'the preface to *Cromwell* shone like the tables of the law on Sinai.' On a purely theatrical level, Hugo's vision of drama in the Shakespearean tradition, combining poetry, historical colour and violent action, looked forward to a bridging of the gap between the melodramas of the boulevards and the classical tragedies of the Théâtre Français. At the end of 1827, *Cromwell* being too vast to stage, that drama had yet to be written.

* He married her in 1833.

2

1828

'Thank you, my friend, for your immortal book,' wrote Alfred de
Vigny to Victor Hugo. 'It is a colossal work . . . *Cromwell* covers the
face of modern tragedy with wrinkles.'

Eighteen months before, Vigny had published his historical novel
Cinq-Mars, the first major work of its kind in France. Set, as *Les Trois
Mousquetaires* was to be, in the time of Cardinal Richelieu, its final scene
portrayed a discussion between Corneille and the poet Milton in which,
reflecting on the Cardinal's appetite for power, Milton forecasts the
emergence in England of a man whose ambition will take him even
further. 'His name,' he says, 'is Cromwell.'

'Our thoughts often coincide, dear Alfred,' wrote Hugo to Vigny,
inviting him to a reading from his play. . . . 'That's partly why I love
you. I have taken the seventeenth century where you left it and have
made the last word of your novel the first one of my play.'

Hugo and Vigny had been friends since 1820, when they had met in
the salon of their mutual friend Emile Deschamps. Hugo, at eighteen,
was already invested with Chateaubriand's title of 'l'Enfant sublime',
Vigny was a young army officer, dreaming of poetry, bored and disillusioned by garrison life. In Hugo he found for the first time a friend
whose aspirations matched his own. A correspondence began between
them, Hugo's letters shy and slightly formal at first, for his background
was bourgeois and Vigny was an aristocrat and four years his senior.
But their friendship soon became more fervent and more equal. Each
published his first volume of poems in 1822. They continued in fraternal rivalry for the next few years, promoting and delighting in one
another's triumphs and judged on an equal footing by the critics.

Hugo and Emile Deschamps visited Vigny in the officers' mess, the
three of them conducting their conversation, amid shouts of laughter,
entirely in alexandrines. When, in 1822, Hugo, after long opposition,
married his boyhood sweetheart, Adèle Foucher, Vigny was a witness
at his wedding. And when in 1825 Vigny announced his marriage to
Lydia Bunbury, daughter of an English sugar-planter, 'simple, good
and gentle as a Tahitian maiden', Hugo sent effusive congratulations:
'The likeness of our lives completes the harmony of our souls. Our
wives will love one another as we already do and we four shall be as
one.'

The hope was not to be fulfilled. The English Lydia and Adèle Hugo had little in common. Successive miscarriages left Lydia a semi-invalid, unable to bear children. The blonde blue-eyed looks that had enchanted Vigny soon disappeared. Fat and ailing, bad at French and after a while forgetful of her own language, she could take little part in the intellectual give and take of romantic circles. Increasingly her husband took her into the *grand monde* of the Faubourg Saint-Germain where the formal manners of the aristocracy served to hide embarrassments.

His fellow writers saw Vigny as a snob. He was indeed an aristocrat, proud of his title and ancient lineage, perhaps more so than his origins warranted. His parents had seen relatives perish on the guillotine. Poor and proud, over-absorbed in their only son, they had imbued in him a sense of caste which, combined with his natural timidity, tended to cut him off from his contemporaries. Through Hugo, in the heady atmosphere of the Cénacle he was able for a time to throw off his reserve and share the excitement of the romantic battle, knowing his creative powers to be at their height.

In 1827 he had finally abandoned his military career in favour of literature. Too proud to put himself forward, he had received no mark of patronage despite his royalist connections in his thirteen years as a soldier. His chivalrous attitude towards the monarchy, like Hugo's, was changing. He had little money of his own. His wife's father, the sugar-planter, had had substantial estates in the West Indies, and Vigny's mother had nourished hopes of 'regilding the family's arms'. But Lydia's dowry proved disappointingly small. Not long afterwards her father had remarried and rapidly produced a second family, thus decreasing the interest, already slight, which he showed in his daughter's affairs. He had no love for his French son-in-law, whose name in conversation he would pretend to have forgotten.*

But outward circumstances left Vigny curiously untouched. He nursed his wife devotedly, he concealed his poverty, receiving his friends, despite the simplicity of his hospitality, with the grace and formality of a *grand seigneur*. He seemed to live upon a loftier plane than his fellow mortals, lost in the realms of poetry and thought. 'Alfred de Vigny', wrote Arsène Houssaye, 'believed himself already in the

* 'At the time,' wrote Sainte-Beuve, 'that Lamartine was secretary at the Embassy in Florence Mr Bunbury was introduced to him and dined with him. During dinner the Englishman mentioned that he had a daughter married to one of the principal French poets. Asked for the name of the poet, he hesitated and could not remember it. Lamartine then ran through a list of the poets of the period and at the mention of each of them the Englishman replied, "No, no. That's not the one." Not until Lamartine came to Alfred de Vigny did he answer, "Ah yes, I rather fancy that's the name".'

Empyrean . . . It is true that he lived on the fifth floor, and thus was nearly in the seventh heaven.'

Alexandre Dumas, in his memoirs, confirms this impression. 'Alfred de Vigny', he wrote, 'was a singular man, polite, affable and gentle in all his dealings, but affecting the most complete other-worldliness—a characteristic that went to perfection with his charming face, framed in long blonde curls like one of those cherubim whose brother he seemed to be . . .' 'What above all astonished Hugo and me', he went on, 'was that Vigny appeared not the least concerned with the grosser needs of our nature which some of us, Hugo and I among them, satisfied not only without shame but with a certain sensual satisfaction. None of us had ever seen Vigny at table. Marie Dorval, who for seven years passed several hours each day at his side, confessed to us with an amazement approaching terror that she had never seen him eat anything but a radish!'

In 1828 neither Marie Dorval, fresh from her triumphs on the boulevards, nor Dumas, a close friend of the future, had yet come into Vigny's life. Sainte-Beuve, however, pursuing poetry and romantic friendships, had made the acquaintance of Vigny that spring. Their first meeting might have been awkward. Two years before, Sainte-Beuve had attacked *Cinq-Mars* in the *Globe* on the grounds of its historical inaccuracy. But that was before he had fallen under Hugo's spell. Hugo's enthusiasm for Vigny's poetry, which Sainte-Beuve scarcely knew, had opened his eyes. 'I made myself forgiven', he wrote, 'by my sincere admiration for his poetry.' Their friendship soon blossomed, forced perhaps too quickly in the hothouse atmosphere of the Cénacle and watered liberally with flattery; for despite their exchanged compliments they eyed one another from the start with distrust, Sainte-Beuve possessive in his attitude to Hugo, Vigny observing, not without regret, the critic's influence on his friend. 'I have just seen Victor Hugo,' he noted in his diary; 'he had with him Sainte-Beuve and two others. Sainte-Beuve is a small, rather ugly man, with a common face and exceedingly round shoulders, who speaks with obsequious reverential grimaces like an old woman; he expresses himself with difficulty but possesses a tremendous fund of information, and a considerable talent for literary criticism. By dint of intelligence he has come to write excellent poetry without himself being an instinctive poet. Full of seeming modesty, he has set himself up as a henchman of Hugo and has been swept into poetry by him; but Hugo, who all his life has been going from one man to another to skim what he can from them, has acquired quantities of knowledge from him which he never had before; for all his airs of being the master he is the pupil.'

Sainte-Beuve was now virtually a member of the Hugo family. He had given up his medical studies at the end of 1827 to devote himself entirely to literature. He would call on the Hugos twice a day, he had his own seat by the fireside. If Hugo were out he would talk to Madame Hugo, placid and welcoming among her children. She was expecting a baby; another son, François-Victor, would be born in October. In the evenings there were expeditions to Mère Saguet's, a vine-clad restaurant outside the town. The menu was simple. The widow Saguet kept a poultry yard; a plate of eggs would stave off the pangs of hunger while she killed a chicken, plucked it and prepared it. This with cheese, washed down by plentiful supplies of white wine, cost only twenty sous. They would return home in the sunset.

To the charm of friendship was added the awakening of the poetic faculty. 'Coming from a purely rationalist and critical school as the *Globe* then was,' wrote Sainte-Beuve, '. . . it was a whole new world for me and I forgot myself there, savouring the sweetness of praises which were never stinted in those circles and giving rein for the first time to poetic and imaginative faculties which till then I had painfully repressed.' He could recognise the falseness and extravagance of certain aspects of romanticism, but the talent he saw around him gave him courage and he set his critical judgement on one side, consoling himself with the thought that these faults would remain as secrets of the family.

In July 1828 Sainte-Beuve's long projected book on the poets of the Pléiade was published. It was a pioneer work: in it he had tried to keep the balance between the poetic standards of his own age and those of another, an act of historical sympathy that would be the key to future works. He had been drawn into the Cénacle as he was writing it, and his description of the innovations and achievements of the poets of the sixteenth century had been coloured by the thought that with Hugo he was participating in a new Renaissance. The *Tableau Historique et Critique de la Poésie Française au XVIe Siècle*, reviving a lyrical tradition that had long been lost, provided the romantics with a literary ancestry.

The *Tableau* ended with a selection from the poetry of Ronsard. On its publication Sainte-Beuve presented Hugo with the magnificent sixteenth-century in-folio copy of Ronsard's poetry from which he had made his choice. The inscription inside it read:

> 'To the greatest lyrical inventor
> in French poetry since Ronsard,
> from Ronsard's most humble commentator,
> S.B.'

The book, with its gilt-edged leaves and white vellum binding, became part of the iconography of the Romantic Movement. It lay on a table in the 'chambre au lys d'or', where visitors could leaf through it and the most distinguished of them, including Vigny, Lamartine and Dumas, inscribe their verses in its ample margins. Sainte-Beuve wrote a sonnet:

> Votre génie est grand, Ami, votre pensée
> Monte, comme Elisée, au char vivant d'Elie . . .

Such high-flown terms were the common coinage of the Cénacle. Its atmosphere was incense-laden. Hugo himself was a master of flattery. To Victor Pavie, who had written a favourable review of his *Odes et Ballades* in a provincial paper the previous year, he wrote:

'I should think nothing of praise which was merely praise. But what I am grateful for in your article is the tremendous talent I find there; what pleases, what charms, what enchants me, is the total revelation of a noble soul, a deep intelligence, a lofty spirit.'

Victor Pavie was twenty, one of the flock of young men who were rallying to Hugo's standard. The doors of his salon were open to receive them. When Pavie, who had never met Hugo, arrived in Paris he made his way to the Rue Notre-Dame-des-Champs. With shaking knees he gave his name to the servant, who carried a child in her arms. He heard his name announced within. Hugo appeared at the door. 'I flung myself into his arms,' wrote Pavie. 'There was a gap of about five minutes during which I spoke without knowing what I was saying, sobbing with enthusiasm and laughing in the midst of my sobs.'

Not all young visitors were so impressed. Alfred de Musset had been only twelve when he was first introduced to Hugo as a school-friend of Madame Hugo's younger brother Paul Foucher. Now a slim and elegant seventeen-year-old, somewhat dandyish, with the febrile air of a 'flower that is already fading',* he was a frequent visitor both to Hugo's salon and to that of Charles Nodier. Lamartine, who first saw him at the Arsenal, described him as habitually silent and modest amidst the noise and chatter of the crowd around him, dreamy-eyed, his delicate mouth undecided between sadness and a smile. But Lamartine's impression reflected the almost religious awe which Musset felt for him. Like all young men of his generation Musset had swooned over Lamartine's *Méditations*, responding intensely to their mood of romantic melancholy. He felt no such reverence for Hugo. Hugo was only eight years older than he, Lamartine twenty; and Hugo, in 1828, was not yet consecrated by a similar success. His modest shyness in front of Lamartine was not repeated in Hugo's presence. But he could

* Juste Olivier: *Paris en 1830.*

not fail to be caught up in the excitement of the romantic struggle. 'Like a soldier who sees his friends charging into gunfire', recalled his brother, 'Alfred felt seized by the desire to try his own powers.' One morning, after an evening of poetry and literary discussion he went round to wake up Sainte-Beuve and with a gaiety that concealed nervousness recited some of his poems to him. 'We have a child of genius among us,' wrote Sainte-Beuve to a friend next day.

*   *   *

Meanwhile the theatrical challenge thrown down in the preface to *Cromwell* had not been forgotten. Some years before, Hugo had written a tragedy, *Amy Robsart*, adapted from Walter Scott's *Kenilworth*. Dissatisfied with it and unwilling to use someone else's ideas, he had set it on one side. Now, in the wake of the Shakespearean triumphs, he decided to revive it, prudently however presenting it as the work of another man, his seventeen-year-old brother-in-law, Paul Foucher.

Delacroix designed the costumes, Hugo himself arranged for its production at the Odéon theatre. The experiment proved a disaster. The first night, February 13th, took place amidst an 'indescribable tumult', the actors hissed and shouted into inaudibility by classicists who, hearing rumours of the play's true source, had come to jeer at the author of *Cromwell*. The play was ignominiously withdrawn a few days later.

Poor Paul Foucher, who had lent his name unwillingly, was in despair. Hugo, honour-bound to defend him, wrote a letter to the papers. He himself, he declared, had been responsible for 'certain words, certain fragments of the play . . . the parts that had been most hissed'—a disingenuous half-confession since the whole play was his own. 'The episode is a little cloudy,' writes a biographer, 'and it cannot be said that Hugo's conduct shines too brightly through the clouds.'

The failure of *Amy Robsart* was a setback, though only a temporary one, for the cause of romantic drama. For Hugo it was a precious lesson. Never again would he go into battle half-prepared. Those ardent young men, so warmly welcomed to his side, would be his cohorts when the moment came.

In March 1828 Alfred de Vigny and Emile Deschamps completed a translation of *Romeo and Juliet*. Hugo was enthusiastic. 'Your *Roméo* is admirable,' he wrote to Vigny; 'it is the *Roméo* of William and yet it is your own. It needed a genius as great as his to translate it as you have done.'

Roméo et Juliette was accepted at the Théâtre Français, a breakthrough less amazing than it at first appeared since Baron Taylor, the director, was an old comrade in arms of Vigny's and a friend of Nodier and

[19]

Hugo. His appointment three years earlier had roused the consternation of the classicists who saw their citadel in danger from within. His
name—he was a naturalised Frenchman, born in Brussels of English
parents—had caused further offence. 'This compatriot of Shakespeare,'
they said, 'despises Corneille, Racine and Molière.'

Their worst fears now seemed realised. The decline in receipts had
strengthened Taylor's hand in opening up the theatre to new influences.
'The revolution will be carried through', wrote Hugo to Deschamps,
'and carried through by Emile and Alfred ... What was doubtful with
Cromwell will be more than sure with *Roméo*.'

The Cénacle rejoiced too soon. Mademoiselle Mars, the natural
candidate for the leading part and not one to relinquish her claims
lightly, was nearing fifty, past the age for Juliet. Vigny, secretly unhappy about the quality of Deschamps' work, showed no inclination
to tackle her opposition or that of other actors. Worse, another *Roméo*
had been accepted at the rival Odéon. The play was set aside indefi-
nitely.

The classicists breathed once more. Vigny turned his attention to a
translation of *Othello*, this time without collaboration, Hugo to the
preparation of a novel and a new collection of poems, *Les Orientales*.
The literary fermentation was intense. 'Victor, Alfred de Vigny, Emile
Deschamps, Sainte-Beuve, Alfred de Musset and I,' wrote Paul Foucher
to a friend, 'are all plunged in work. Victor is like a column in the
midst of us all and from time to time throws us an "Orientale" like a
paving stone dropped upon ants.'

But the first real breach in the classical defences would be made by
none of these, but by an outsider at that moment completely unknown,
a former clerk in the office of the king's cousin, the Duc d'Orléans. His
name was Alexandre Dumas.

*　　*　　*

Alexandre Dumas was twenty-six. He had come to Paris with no
money and huge ambitions four years earlier. His father, the son of a
West Indian slave and the Marquis de la Pailleterie, had been a general
under Napoleon, renowned for his feats of bravery, but had fallen foul
of the Emperor and died disgraced. From him Dumas had inherited his
size—he was over six foot—and his physical exuberance; from him too
came his head of crinkly black hair contrasting strangely with pale blue
eyes alight with intelligence and wit.

For Dumas, as for Berlioz, the Shakespearean performances had
been a revelation. For the first time, he wrote, he had seen real passions
on the stage, animating men and women of flesh and blood. He felt like
a blind man who has just received his sight. He perceived that 'in the

theatrical world everything emanates from Shakespeare, just as in the real world everything emanates from the sun . . . I realised in fact that, after God, Shakespeare had created more than any other human being.' From that moment he saw his vocation clear.

He had already had a pair of burlesques performed in the vaudeville theatre and had tried his hand, less successfully, at poetry and a tragedy. In his spare moments as a clerk, supplementing a happy-go-lucky education, he had studied history and literature voraciously. Shakespearean drama, or rather his interpretation of it, would bring the threads of these studies together and satisfy the appetite for violence and excitement which the son of a Napoleonic hero had in his blood.

No novel by Dumas could better the story of the next eighteen months—his struggles, his setbacks, his final astounding success as a dramatist—and no d'Artagnan could make a more delightful hero than Dumas is of his own memoirs. If truth and fiction sometimes mingle, his personality is large enough to impose its own pattern on events.

Dumas had his first dramatic subject waiting. At the autumn exhibition of the Salon a few days previously he had been struck by one of the most discussed exhibits, a bas-relief by a woman sculptor depicting the assassination of Monaldeschi, favourite of Queen Christina of Sweden, in the Galerie des Cerfs at Fontainebleau. Dumas knew nothing of the queen or of her murdered lover, but the episode looked promising. Borrowing a biographical dictionary, he read up all he could on the subject, his imagination taking fire as he went on. His drama would be called *Christine*.

In less than six months, seizing every idle moment in his office hours and working through the night at home, he had completed a five-act play in verse. 'I felt as embarrassed,' he wrote, 'as a poor girl who's had a baby out of wedlock.' What should he do with this bastard, conceived outside all academic auspices? It seemed too vigorous to smother, its aspirations went far beyond the theatres of the boulevards. The Théâtre Français? There were hundreds of plays waiting to be read there; without a letter to Baron Taylor, the director, he might have to wait a year for a reading.

Dumas knew no one of influence at the Théâtre Français but he had once, by chance, met Taylor's friend Charles Nodier. The circumstances had been typically eccentric. At a performance of *Le Vampire*, a ridiculous melodrama, four years before, he had fallen into conversation with his neighbour in the interval, a charming and erudite gentleman with whom he had talked agreeably of vampires, old books and cookery. This gentleman, in the course of the third act, was forcibly evicted from the theatre for hissing the performance. The disturber of the peace, Dumas read in the papers next day, had been none other than the celebrated Charles Nodier, co-author of the play, though whether he was hissing his own work, his colleague's, or the actors, remained a mystery.

Would Nodier remember the episode? It was barely possible, but, failing any other introduction, Dumas wrote to him, recalling *Le Vampire*, his hisses and their conversation, and begging his help for *Christine*. Nodier did not reply, but a few days later a letter arrived from Taylor inviting him to read his play aloud and offering an appointment at seven in the morning in his apartment, his only moment in a crowded day.

Dumas' memoirs describe this memorable first meeting. He arrived at Taylor's flat to find himself forestalled by another aspiring playwright who held the director trapped, like Marat, in his bath while he read him, at seemingly endless length, a five-act tragedy. By the time it had reached its weary close and its persistent author been despatched, the bath-water was cold. Taylor, whose teeth were chattering, jumped back into bed. Dumas politely offered to return some other time.

'Ah no,' said Taylor, 'since you're here . . .'

'Then,' said Dumas, 'I will read you the first act and if it tires or bores you I will stop.'

'You've more compassion than your *confrère*,' said Baron Taylor; 'that's a good sign.'

With a trembling voice almost inaudible from nervousness, Dumas read the first act.

'Shall I go on?' he asked timidly.

'But yes, but yes,' said Baron Taylor. 'Upon my word it's very good.'

Dumas read on with growing courage. His interest turning to enthusiasm as he listened, Taylor himself demanded the third act, then the fourth, then the fifth.

In less than a week, with Taylor's recommendation behind it, *Christine* had been accepted by the committee of the Théâtre Français. But Dumas' joy was short-lived. He was soon to discover, he wrote, that 'in the theatre, contrary to real life, all joys belong to giving birth and that after birth the pains begin'. Between acceptance and performance at the Théâtre Français, above all for an unknown author, lay a minefield of obstruction and intrigue. Taylor, despite his title of director, was a constitutional monarch presiding in the midst of backstage factions. Like *Roméo et Juliette*, *Christine* was abandoned in mid-rehearsal.

But Dumas had tasted blood. He had come so far so quickly. There was glory to be won on the stage; he would seize it as his father had seized it in battle. In two months of furious work he completed a second play, this time in prose and of a far more sensational kind. Chance had once more provided the theme, an anecdote of the court of Henri III which he had glimpsed in a book left open on a colleague's desk. Dumas plunged into the memoirs of the sixteenth century. Assassinations and assignation, the wiles of Catherine de Medici, the king's rivalry with his cousin the Duc de Guise, provided vivid material for a play in which physical violence, as opposed to the purely moral agonies of classical tragedy, played a prominent part.

This time there was no dragging of feet at the Théâtre Français. The summer season had been disastrous. Taylor, attacked by the classicists on one side, was under still greater pressure on the other. Without a success, and a resounding one, the theatre faced bankruptcy. Classical tragedies, however correct, were unlikely to provide one. Dumas meanwhile had taken his precautions. Though he did not yet aspire to the Cénacle, he had friends in literary circles and had been at pains to enlist the support of journalists and actors at preliminary readings. On September 17th his play was received 'with acclamation' at the Théâtre Français; the first performance was planned for February 1829.

Though it bore little signs of the Shakespearean inspiration that he claimed for it, though its view of history was crude and highly coloured, there was no mistaking its speed and theatrical effect. Dumas, a born dramatist, had sprung into the arena fully armed, with his second play. 'I have written fifty plays since *Henri III et sa Cour*,' he wrote later, 'but none have been better constructed.'

3

1829

The publicity surrounding Dumas' play, and his frequent absences from work, had earned him an ultimatum from the director of the Duc d'Orléans' office, one which, despite a personal plea from Dumas, the Duke himself upheld. The duties of a clerk were incompatible with a theatrical career; he must choose between the two. Dumas, whose choice was never in question, found himself abruptly suspended from his post. The salary, now withdrawn, had been meagre enough and stretched to its limits, for Dumas was already responsible for two establishments, the rooms which he shared with his widowed mother and those he provided for Catherine Lebay, a pretty seamstress by whom he had had a son, now four years old—the future Alexandre Dumas *fils*. Fidelity was not in Dumas' nature and he had long moved on to other conquests, but he was a devoted son, and in his careless, cheerful way a loving father.

Penniless, his prospects of a safe career abandoned, he was nonetheless able to obtain a loan on the manuscript of his play. The immediate problems of existence were solved, but the long-term ones remained. Dumas' mother, less sanguine than her son, was pitifully anxious; this anxiety, at the beginning of February, was enough to precipitate a stroke, leaving her paralysed and unable to speak. Dumas spent the last few days before the first night between rehearsals and his mother's bedside.

The first performance was due to take place on February 11th. On the eve of that day, Dumas requested an interview with the Duc d'Orléans.

'Oh, it's you, Monsieur Dumas,' said the Duke. 'What good wind brings you here?'

'I've come to ask you for a favour, Monseigneur, or rather for justice.'

And Dumas requested his former employer to attend the first performance to judge whether he had condemned him too hastily in dismissing him.

'Alas,' said the Duke, 'that is impossible. I have twenty or thirty princes and princesses dining with me tomorrow. We sit down at table at six o'clock and *Henri III* begins at seven.'

'If Monseigneur would advance the hour of his dinner by one hour

I will put back *Henri III* by one hour. Monseigneur would then have three hours to assuage the hunger of his guests.'

'But where would I put them? I have only three boxes.'

'I have begged the administration not to dispose of the gallery until I have seen your highness.'

The Duke, intrigued, gave his consent.

The theatre was packed on the morrow. Seats had been sold out for weeks. Hugo and Vigny, who had asked for places, sat in the box of Dumas' sister. Thirty princes and princesses, bedecked with diamonds and decorations, filled the first tier of the theatre. Dumas himself had a small box next to the stage.

The curtain rose. 'Never have I felt such a sensation as that of the cold air upon my dripping forehead,' he recalled. The first two acts went well, but it was the third act which would decide the fortunes of the play, its high spot being the scene when the Duc de Guise, forcing his wife to give a false assignation to her lover, crushes her arm with his iron gauntlet. This brutality, hitherto unthinkable at the Théâtre Français, was greeted with cries of terror and applause.

Dumas rushed home to embrace his mother, alas unconscious of her son's success, and returned to a 'mounting delirium' in the theatre. Madame Malibran, the great opera singer, was leaning right out of her box, clutching a pillar to stop herself from falling. When the play was ended and the author's name announced the entire audience, including the Duc d'Orléans, rose to its feet to cheer him. People crowded to congratulate him. Victor Hugo, whom till then he had not been privileged to meet, came up to take his hand.

'Ah,' cried Dumas, 'at last I am one of you!'

'I was thrilled by my success,' he wrote, 'but what rendered it most precious was the right it had won me to take that hand.'

The next day Dumas woke up famous. His mother's room was filled with flowers. By lunch-time he had repaid his loan and sold the rights of his play for 6,000 francs. But that evening he found consternation at the theatre. The censor's office had suspended the play. Charles X himself had sent for the Duc d'Orléans; he had been told, he complained, that the portraits of Henri III and his cousin the Duc de Guise were based on the characters of himself and the Duc d'Orléans.

'You have been deceived, Sire,' replied the Duke, 'and that for three reasons: the first is that I do not beat my wife; the second is that the Duchess has not made me a cuckold; and the third is that your majesty has no more loyal subject than myself.'

The censor's office was persuaded to withdraw the ban, and the play resumed its triumphant career. The literary world flung open its doors to Dumas. David d'Angers, who specialised in romantic portraits, made a medallion of his head, and Eugène Devéria a lithograph which was displayed side by side with those of Vigny and Hugo in the shop windows of Paris.

The classicists meanwhile denounced the desecration of the Théâtre Français. Rumour had it that after the first night of *Henri III*, when the lights in the foyer had been lowered, a group of young romantics had danced a wild fandango round the statue of Racine to the chanted refrain of 'Bury Racine!'. Seven leading men of letters sent an urgent petition to the king, begging him to withstand the invasion of romantic drama and to uphold the ancient dignity of the national theatre. 'Sire, the danger is already great! In a few-months it will be beyond redress.'

The king's reply was short and witty:

'Messieurs, I can do nothing in this matter. I have only, like all Frenchmen, a seat in the pit.'

*   *   *

Hugo was well pleased with Dumas' success. 'It seems to me an excellent transition,' he wrote to Victor Pavie. 'After the setback of *Amy Robsart* nothing is more desirable than an attempt of this kind . . . The breach is made. We will pass through.'

The first month of 1829 had seen the prodigious success of Hugo's *Les Orientales*. Here was the glowing Orient of romantic painting, beloved by Delacroix, here were the sunsets of the Rue Notre-Dame-des-Champs, the light-touched clouds taking on the shapes of domes and minarets, here was a metrical virtuosity which owed something to Sainte-Beuve's studies of the Pléiade. 'Art has nothing to do with restrictions, gags or manacles,' wrote Hugo in his preface. 'It bids you go, and leaves you free to wander in the great garden of poetry where there are no forbidden fruit.' While the classicists were condemning the rhythmical liberties which followed this pronouncement his novel, *Le Dernier Jour d'un Condamné*, appeared, as black and harrowing as *Les Orientales* had been radiant. The macabre was in fashion, but Hugo's horror of the death penalty was deeply felt and the novel, 'an agony of three hundred pages' describing a man's last hours before the guillotine, was the first of his many pleas for reform.

In April came the turn of Sainte-Beuve. His *Vie, Poésies et Pensées de Joseph Delorme* appeared on the 4th. 'Read, my dear friend', he had written to Hugo, 'these few miserable pages . . . If you genuinely feel there is no scruple or shame in revealing these nakednesses of the soul, say so and I will deliver them to the public, if only to give it a new sensation.'

Joseph Delorme, a medical student devoured by melancholy and poetic longings, dies young of an incurable disease, leaving behind him

his notebook and his poems—a sad case of 'mal du siècle'. The sorrows
of Joseph—a 'Jacobin sawbones sort of Werther' as Guizot described
him—were hard to take seriously, but his poems were not. Low-keyed,
domestic, with none of the sweep or range of the poet's greater contemporaries, they sounded a note of careful, sometimes painful realism
which was new in French verse. Two were inscribed to Victor Hugo;
another, uncharacteristically eloquent, hymned the glories of the Cénacle
and its young leader.

> Parmi vous un génie a grandi sous l'orage,
> Jeune et fort: sur son front s'est imprimé l'outrage
> En éclairs radieux;
> Mais il dépose ici son sceptre et le repousse,
> Sa gloire sans rayons se fait aimable et douce
> Et rit à tous les yeux.
>
> Oh! qu'il chante longtemps! car son luth nous
>   entraîne,
> Nous rallie et nous guide, et nous tiendrons
>   l'arène
> Tant qu'il retentira;
> Deux ou trois tours encore, aux sons de sa
>   trompette
> Aux éclats de sa voix que tout un choeur répète,
> Jéricho tombera . . .

Sainte-Beuve's love and admiration for his friend were as strong as
ever, but there was a new element in his relationship with the Hugos.
While Hugo was striding forward to new triumphs and achievements,
Adèle, the adored and much sung wife, found herself inevitably somewhat neglected. Tied at home, occupied with her three small children,
she found consolation in the company of Sainte-Beuve, who treated
her as an intellectual equal and who seemed to treasure his glimpses of
domestic life. Sometimes she would tease him about some supposed
love affair, sometimes they would discuss religion. Adèle Hugo was
devout, Sainte-Beuve had religious yearnings. Later he would make
light of them: 'I have created a little Christian mythology in my time;
it has evaporated. It was like the swan of Leda for me, a means of
arriving at fair ladies and of slipping into their love,' but this was the
cynicism of hindsight. Meanwhile, these long discursive conversations,
these talks of ideals and the infinite, were the greatest pleasure of his days.

Hugo, so possessive towards his wife in general, had little fear of her
friendship with this ugly sandy-haired young man who was proving

invaluable as his ally, rallying the *Globe* to support *Les Orientales*, confirming his *rapprochement* with the liberals. For the leader of the Cénacle, even while he gathered new followers, was bringing upon himself the full fury of the classical opposition. 'Avec impunité', declared a pamphlet, 'les Hugos font des vers.'

Hugo was preparing a new theatrical coup, the final blow that would bring down the citadel of classicism. On June 1st he began his *Marion de Lorme*, subtitled *Un duel sous Richelieu*; on June 20th, starting at daybreak and writing till dawn the next morning, he wrote the fourth act; on June 24th the play was completed.

A reading was arranged in the 'chambre au lys d'or'. The flower of the romantic school were there, among them Balzac, Delacroix, Vigny, Dumas, Musset, Sainte-Beuve, Emile Deschamps and his brother Antony, Boulanger and the Devéria brothers. Edouard Turquety, a young disciple, describes that memorable evening:

'You can imagine my enthusiasm. I was twenty years old; I was received with open arms by the most famous poets, and after all Hugo was a man of genius. I felt as though I was present at a reading of *Le Cid*; I even confess that I did not blush to say as much . . . Little Sainte-Beuve circled the mighty Victor . . . The illustrious Alexandre Dumas waved his enormous arms with boundless enthusiasm. I remember that after the reading he seized the poet and, lifting him up with herculean force, cried: "We will carry you to glory!" David d'Angers, the sculptor, looked thoughtful; as for Emile Deschamps he applauded before even hearing the words and in his flirtatious way kept surreptitiously eyeing the ladies of the party. Refreshments were served: I can still see the immense Dumas stuffing down cakes and repeating with his mouth full, "Superb! Superb!" This comedy, which so gaily succeeded the sombre drama, did not finish until two in the morning.'

The play was received with acclamation at the Théâtre Français. On July 17th, eight days after the reading of *Marion de Lorme*, the Cénacle re-assembled, this time for a reading of Alfred de Vigny's *Othello*. 'On Friday the 17th, at exactly seven-thirty,' wrote Vigny to Sainte-Beuve, 'the Moor of Venice will live and die before you; should you wish to seat the shade of Joseph Delorme at this funeral banquet his place is prepared, as is that of Banquo.'

'The evening was very brilliant,' wrote Turquety, 'nothing but counts and barons were announced.' Alfred de Musset, a dashing figure in tight sky-blue trousers, gave the signal for the applause. Hugo was 'at his post'. '*Othello*, Alfred and Shakespeare,' he wrote, 'here is a powerful trinity of genius.'

Othello too was accepted at the Théâtre Français, where it was to follow Hugo's play.

But the censor's office, which had let pass *Henri III*, baulked at *Marion de Lorme*: not only was Louis XIII, a direct ancestor of the king, ridiculed in the play, but in the figure of a monarch ruled by a priest, the world might see an allusion to Charles X himself. Hugo went to plead with the Minister of the Interior. In vain he declared the purity of his intentions, the strictly historical sense in which he had portrayed the king; the Minister was obdurate.

Hugo went on to intercede with the king himself after requesting and obtaining a private audience. Charles was gracious but unyielding. It was August 7th. Two days later he would appoint as his chief minister the ultra-reactionary Prince de Polignac and thus lose his last chance of a compromise with the forces of liberalism. From then on, with a mystical faith in Providence and the smiling serenity of somnambulists, king and minister would move forward to their doom. They had less than a year to rule. In a long poem, written eleven years later, Hugo described his interview: the old monarch, white-haired, bowed with years and kingship, the young poet pleading the cause of liberty in art, the tranquillity and seeming permanence of the royal ensemble.

The king's refusal was softened next day by an offer of an increase in Hugo's royal pension. Hugo, with dignity and considerable publicity, declined it.

With the suppression of *Marion de Lorme*, the way was open for *Othello* on whose fortunes the hopes of romantic drama now rested. Rehearsals began immediately and the fastidious Vigny began to taste the bitterness of backstage intrigues. Cold and distant, he lacked the right manner to cajole the members of the Comédie Française and at one point, exasperated, threatened to withdraw an intransigent Iago from his role. But the casting of Mademoiselle Mars as Desdemona was a powerful card in his hand and the friendship of Baron Taylor, who borrowed from the next year's budget to mount a lavish production with elaborate scenery including a gothic palace and a gothic chamber, did much to lighten his difficulties.

Hugo saw these preparations with mixed feelings. Fraternal rivalry was all very well, but it seemed for the moment as though the role that he had claimed with *Marion de Lorme* was falling to Vigny. True, Dumas had led the way with his *Henri III*, but Dumas was not a poet, and his play had been in prose.

With the same prodigious energy that he had shown before Hugo set to work on another play. A week after the rejection of *Marion de Lorme* he dined with Charles Nodier and Baron Taylor. Baron Taylor was going away.

'When will you be back?' asked Hugo.

'At the end of the month.'

'That gives me a little more than three weeks. Well then, call together a committee for the first of October and I will read them something.'

In three weeks Hugo had finished *Hernani*.

Once more the Cénacle gathered for a reading in the 'chambre au lys d'or'. 'All the leaders of romanticism were there,' wrote Auguste Barbier. 'One alone had delayed his appearance. It was the author of *Eloa*.* At last he arrived and I saw passing through the ranks of bearded, long-haired *Jeunes-France* a gentleman of perfect elegance, with a black coat and tie and white waistcoat. His figure was slender, his features pale and regular: thin lips, a slightly aquiline nose, grey-blue eyes under a fine forehead framed in blonde hair, an expression of great distinction. The reading of the play began. The poet read well, but his intonation was disagreeable. His voice, composed of two tones, the deep and the shrill, shifted continually from one to another, which to some extent destroyed the effect. Nevertheless the work, full of beautiful verses and chivalrous sentiments scattered in profusion through a somewhat improbable story, produced an enthusiasm difficult to describe. When the reading was finished, everyone went to congratulate the author; and among the crowd I saw the bard of *Eloa*, still with a cold and reserved expression, come forward to clasp the hand of his friend and confrère, after which he discreetly eclipsed himself.'

It was the first sign of a rift between Hugo and Vigny. For some days the situation seemed complicated. Should *Hernani*, which had replaced *Marion de Lorme*, have precedence over *Othello* at the Théâtre Français? *Marion de Lorme* had been accepted first, but then it could be argued that *Othello* was the replacement for *Roméo et Juliette*, accepted but postponed the year before. At the Théâtre Français the actors, who had little sympathy for Vigny's lofty ways, would have been glad to see him passed over. The affair reached the press. The *Globe* preached moderation: a translation of Shakespeare, however distinguished, could in no way destroy the impact of an original work. Let *Hernani* cede to Shakespeare; the one would prepare the way for the other.

In the tone of a hidalgo from *Hernani* Hugo put an end to the discussion. 'I have always understood that whatever the date of its acceptance *Othello* should go before *Hernani*, *Hernani* before *Othello*, never,' he announced in a letter to the *Globe*.

'People are trying to disunite us,' wrote Hugo privately to Vigny,

---

* Alfred de Vigny's long narrative poem *Eloa* was published in 1824. Eloa, an angel 'born from a tear of Christ', sacrifices her place in heaven out of pity and love for Satan. Hugo reviewed the poem in 1824. Ten years later, when friendship had cooled, he reprinted the review, with a simple change of title, as an essay on *Paradise Lost*.

'but I will prove to you on the day of *Othello* that I am more than ever your good and devoted friend.'

* * *

October 24th was the first night of *Othello*. For two months Vigny had been preparing his forces. 'It is the cause of youth,' he wrote to a supporter, 'it is one liberty the more we stand to gain.' The theatre was crowded with zealous romantics, Hugo himself, with his father-in-law at his side, conducting the troops.

Vigny had need of all their support. Shakespeare in English, the words only dimly understood, was one thing, Shakespeare in French was another. The word *mouchoir* created an uproar among the classicists: never before had an object of such vulgarity been mentioned on the stage of the Théâtre Français; previous translations, recoiling from such grossness, had replaced the fatal handkerchief with a diamond bandeau. Othello's blackness was another shock: earlier, sweetened versions had shown him as merely olive-skinned.

'For the first time,' wrote Dumas, 'one heard the roars of African jealousy, we shuddered with emotion at the sobs of that terrible rage . . . Never have I seen anything more dramatic than that great African figure, crossing the theatre like a ghost in the night, draped in his flowing burnous, murmuring in a sombre voice, arms outstretched towards the room of Desdemona:

> . . . Attends, femme! J'arrive!
> Ton sang, bientôt versé par mon bras satisfait,
> Va couler sur ce lit qu'a souillé ton forfait!

In the teeth of catcalls and derisive laughter the romantics, outshouting and outnumbering the classicists, were able to carry the evening. '*Othello* has succeeded,' wrote Hugo to Sainte-Beuve, 'not startlingly, but as much as it could and thanks to us. My conduct on this occasion has completely restored Vigny and our Shakespeareans.'

Vigny had had 'his evening' as he liked to call it. It was a victory very different from Dumas', one whose real importance lay not in such supposed audacities as Desdemona's death on stage but in its poetic style. The solemn measure of the alexandrine had suited the heroes of classical tragedy; romantic drama, with its great variety of mood and character, demanded a more supple instrument. 'We have not the good fortune', wrote Vigny in his preface to the play, 'to be able to mingle prose, blank verse and rhyme in the same scene; in England you can range through these three octaves and they have a harmony which cannot be attained in French (for lack of phonetic accents). To translate them if

[31]

was necessary to unbend the alexandrine, widening its scope from the easiest familiarity to the heights of lyricism: it is this that I have attempted to do.'

The success of *Othello* seemed to have brought Hugo and Vigny together again. Vigny's diary, nonetheless, showed a growing disenchantment. 'The Hugo that I loved is no more,' he wrote. 'He was somewhat fanatical in religious devotion and royalism, chaste as a young girl, a little shy as well; it suited him; we loved him like that. Now he loves ribald talk and has become a liberal: it does not become him.'

Vigny kept his reservations to himself. Not all Hugo's friends were so restrained. In November, under the title 'La Camaraderie Littéraire', Henri de Latouche, an ally from earlier days, wrote an attack on the Cénacle and its atmosphere of mutual admiration. 'Since we have all become geniuses,' he commented, 'talent has become exceptionally rare.' And Charles Nodier, soon after, in an article on Byron and Moore, used the occasion to compare Hugo's work unfavourably with theirs: 'There are people who think . . . that natural genius, with all its riches, can develop in the midst of polite conversation, with no other stimulant but the desire for fame.'

'You too, Charles!' wrote Hugo. 'I would give much not to have read yesterday's *Quotidienne*. The shock which uproots an old and profound friendship is one of the most terrible one can experience.'

'A terrible storm is building up round me,' he wrote to Sainte-Beuve, 'and the hatred of all this low journalism is so strong that I am written off as worthless.'

To the hostility of the press, of classicists and former friends, was added that of the actors of the Théâtre Français. Though they had been happy enough to play a bad turn on Vigny, they had nonetheless been half-hearted about taking on *Hernani*. The committee had accepted the play in its entirety, less out of enthusiasm than because the admiring cries of Hugo's friends, whom he had wisely brought to the reading, had drowned the objections of the actors. Hugo's duel with Mademoiselle Mars, as recounted in Dumas' memoirs, has become a legend.

Dumas had had his own troubles with Mademoiselle Mars. For years she had been the unchallenged queen of the Théâtre Français, excelling in comedy, and, though well past forty, in the role of *ingénues*. Less apt for the violent passions demanded by romantic drama, she was ready to battle with her authors in order to adjust her parts to suit her talents. On stage her voice was light and silvery, off stage it took on a steelier tone. She had a solid reputation for bad comradeship among her fellow players, admitting no rival. Dumas' attentions to a younger actress during the rehearsals for *Henri III* had not gone unnoticed; she described

him as 'stinking of nigger', flinging open her windows when he visited
her dressing-room. But whereas Dumas was exuberant and quick to
react, Hugo remained cold, calm and imperturbably polite whatever the
provocations. And there were many. There was the question above all
of the line, 'Vous êtes mon lion! superbe et généreux', which Mademoiselle Mars, as the heroine Dõna Sol, addressed to Monsieur Firmin
playing the character of Hernani.

Each day the same comedy would take place. In the midst of the
rehearsal she would stop and, shading her eyes with her hand, make a
pretence of searching for the author, whom she could very well see, in
the auditorium.

'Monsieur Hugo,' she would ask, 'is Monsieur Hugo there?'
'I am here, Madame,' replied Hugo, rising.
'Ah, very good! Thank you . . . Tell me, Monsieur Hugo . . .'
'Madame?'
'I have to say this line here:
    Vous êtes mon lion! superbe et généreux!'
'Yes, Madame; Hernani says to you:
    Hélas! j'aime pourtant d'une amour bien profonde!—
    Ne pleure pas, mourons plutôt! Que n'ai-je un monde?
    Je te le donnerais! Je suis bien malheureux!
and you reply:
    Vous êtes mon lion! superbe et généreux!'
'And do you like that, Monsieur Hugo?'
'What?'
'Vous êtes mon lion!'
'I wrote it, Madame, so I must have thought it was right.'
'So you stick then to your lion?'
'I stick to it and I don't stick to it, Madame; find me something
better and I will put it in its place.'
'It's not for me to find it; I'm not the author.'
'Very well then, Madame, since that is so, let us simply leave it as it
was written . . .'

The next day the dialogue would repeat itself, Hugo's exasperation
mounting till one day, with cold formality, he demanded the return of
her role.

'You are a woman of great talent, I know,' he added, 'but there is
something of which you seem to be unaware and which, that being so,
I shall tell you: it is that I also, Madame, am a person of great talent.
Take that as said and deal with me accordingly.'

Mademoiselle Mars gave way to a superior power—which did not
prevent her, when the first night came, from replacing 'mon lion' with
'mon seigneur'.

The future production continued to be attacked on all sides, by royalists who regarded Hugo as a deserter, by liberals as yet unconvinced of his sincerity. The censor's office, unable to ban the play and hoping to kill it by ridicule, leaked out scenes and verses which were passed from hand to hand in classical salons and parodied in the press. Sainte-Beuve, hitherto Hugo's loyal trumpeter, showed himself curiously reserved. Only the young, to whom Hugo was a leader and not a rival, were wholehearted in their enthusiasm.

That winter was exceptionally cold. The Seine was frozen from December to February. Hugo wore slippers to the theatre in order not to break his leg in crossing the bridges. The actors shivered in rehearsals, rushing through their lines in order to return to the warmth of the foyer. Scene-painters, unable to use their vast ill-heated studios in the cold, were held up. Delays accumulated: the first performance was put back till February 1830. Both sides, romantic and classical, used the time to consolidate their forces.

In the midst of rehearsals, controversy, financial worries—Hugo's father had died recently and there were complicated negotiations about his estate—the joyous gatherings of the Cénacle, for the time being, ceased.

One evening however shone out brilliantly. On December 24th, before a chosen audience in his father's house, Alfred de Musset made his literary début with a reading from his forthcoming volume *Contes d'Espagne et d'Italie*. He had read his poems elsewhere: between two waltzes at Charles Nodier's, in the salon of Eugène Devéria, who sketched him in fancy dress, in the satin-sleeved doublet of a mediaeval page, and in the 'chambre au lys d'or'. In a gentle tilt at Hugo his poem 'Mardoche' described that evening hour.

> Où (quand par le brouillard la chatte rôde et pleure),
> Monsieur Hugo va voir mourir Phébus le blond . . .

But this was his real début: the poems themselves were to be published in January. He had learnt from his elders in the Cénacle the importance of gathering the influence of the salons behind him. Young, charming, he brought to his reading a verve and gaiety, a healthy disrespect for their Olympian airs, putting his poetry *en déshabillé*, carrying fantasy to the point of insolence. His famous 'Ballade à la Lune', with its image of the moon not as some silvery goddess but as the dot on an 'i', was received with delight:

> C'était, dans la nuit brune,
> Sur le clocher jauni,

La lune,
Comme un point sur un i . . .

'I can see him now as he made his entry into the literary world,'. wrote Sainte-Beuve, 'first in the little circle of Victor Hugo, then of Alfred de Vigny and the Deschamps brothers. What a début! What nonchalance and grace! From his first verses—his "Andalouse", his "Juana", his "Don Paez"—what surprise and rapture he excited round him. This is how the spring comes; a very springtime of poetry burst into life before our eyes. He was not yet eighteen: his forehead was masculine and proud, the roses of boyhood bloomed on his cheeks, his nostrils quivered with desire, his step rang firm, his eyes were lifted high as if sure of victory and filled with the pride of life. No man, at first sight, gave a more vivid impression of adolescent genius.'

[4]

1830

Revolution was in the air. The liberals were gathering their forces. The liberal press, indignant at the appointment of Polignac as chief minister, was attacking the government with unprecedented violence. The king meanwhile continued in his chosen path, sustained by his trust in God and in his divine right to rule. His chief minister shared his faith: he claimed to have heard voices and to have been visited by the Virgin. 'There is no such thing as political experience,' wrote the Duke of Wellington, no liberal himself; 'with the example of James II before him Charles X is setting up a government by priests, for priests and through priests.' Significantly at that moment, the newly founded liberal paper, the *National*, was devoting a series to the English revolution of 1688.

The theatrical revolution accomplished by *Hernani* could be seen as the dress rehearsal for the political storm about to break: the sense of unity, illusory though it turned out to be, between the cause of artistic and political freedom, heightened the already intense emotions connected with the play to an extraordinary pitch. Hugo, with his brilliant sense of publicity, knew how to turn these passions to good account. For the opening performance he had decided to dispense with the claque traditionally provided by the theatre, whose sympathies might be suspect, and to recruit his own supporters from the students of the Latin Quarter—poets, painters, musicians, sculptors, architects, all young, all ardent in the cause of liberty and in their devotion to the man they regarded as France's greatest poet.

Out of a total of fifteen hundred seats, Hugo had been given four hundred—the orchestra pit, most of the parterre and the second row of the galleries. The weeks before the opening night were hectic. Hugo's apartment was invaded by crowds of young recruits eager to play their part in the great battle. Madame Hugo presided over the plan of the theatre, her habitual lassitude giving place to energy and enthusiasm as she welcomed and encouraged and gave out the red tickets marked with the enigmatic Spanish word *Hierro* (iron) which Hugo had prepared for his supporters.

Gone was the peaceful haven where Sainte-Beuve had spent so many afternoons in tranquil conversation. Now when he came to call he found that Hugo was absent at rehearsals, and that Madame Hugo, surrounded by young men and lavish in her attentions to them, had scarcely time to greet him.

Sainte-Beuve had never been happy about *Hernani*. He distrusted, though he could not hope to equal, its soaring eloquence, he disliked the theatricality of its emotions. He could not be indifferent to the magnificence of the poetry or the lyrical beauty of the love scenes—in which Hugo drew on memories of his first courtship of Adèle—but to him, lacking confidence in his own creative powers and confused in his emotions, they seemed more a threat than an inspiration.

Hugo, absorbed in the task ahead, confident of the support of the man he had come to regard as his dearest friend, was too egoistic and too occupied to sense that a storm was brewing. Sainte-Beuve could not contain himself. Six days before the performance, his jealousy and irritation broke out.

'It is impossible for me at this moment,' he wrote to Hugo, 'to write anything on *Hernani* that would not be detestable in form and substance. I am blasé about *Hernani* . . .

'When I think of what has been happening in recent days, your life at the mercy of all comers, new hatreds roused, old and noble friends disappearing, fools and idiots replacing them, when I see the lines and frowns on your face which are not merely the result of great thoughts, I cannot but feel afflicted, I cannot but regret the past and, saluting you with a gesture, creep off to hide myself I know not where; Bonaparte the Consul was more sympathetic to me than Napoleon the Emperor.'

And then as an afterthought, scribbled furiously in the margin of the last page, a postscript which exposed the core of his resentment:

'And what of *Madame*? She whose name should never echo on your lyre save before an audience on bended knees, even she is exposed to profane eyes all day long, giving out theatre tickets to more than eighty young men whom yesterday she scarcely knew. That chaste and charming intimacy, the true prize of friendship, is irrevocably deflowered by the mob; the word devotion is prostituted, worldly expediency and stratagems carry all before them!!!'

But Hugo, harassed on all sides, had no time to look for undertones nor could Sainte-Beuve, despite the turmoil of his feelings, bring himself publicly to desert his friend at this critical hour. He would not write in favour of the play but he continued to act the role of 'faithful Achates' in the final days; he was at Hugo's side for the epic battle of the opening night.

February 25th, 1830. By midday Hugo's troops had begun to gather outside the door of the theatre, four hundred young men, bearded, long haired, clothed in mediaeval doublets, in sweeping Rubens hats, in mysterious Spanish cloaks, in anything except the current fashion. The watchword ran from man to man: '*Hierro*! Death to the periwigs!' It had been agreed that they should take their places in the theatre before the public; for fear of being late they had assembled several hours too early. The theatre door was still shut. Curious crowds began to gather, the classicists among them picking up the sweepings from the theatre to throw at the barbarian invaders, Balzac, as Madame Hugo recalled, being struck by a cabbage stump. The romantics refused to be roused; retaliation would have brought the police and risked the success of their mission.

At three o'clock the doors of the theatre were opened and, having received them, were firmly locked again. The interior was unlit, shadowy and cavernous, recalled Théophile Gautier, like an engraving by Piranesi; there were four hours to wait in the gloom before the doors were re-opened. Places were allotted, the prudent who had brought supplies began to picnic off bread and ham and garlic sausage, the time passed merrily with songs, with recitations of Hugo's poetry, with imitations of the animals in the ark. Unfortunately, however, during this long wait, the doors to the cloakrooms remained locked, the attendants having not yet arrived, and those who could contain themselves no longer were forced to seek relief in dark corners. At seven o'clock the great gas chandeliers were lit and the dark corners were dark no longer; the general public began to arrive, the ladies picking up their satin-shod feet in disgust, their nostrils further offended by the pervasive smell of garlic sausage.

When Hugo arrived he was at once informed of the scandal. He hurried to see Mademoiselle Mars and found her furious. 'Fine friends you've got!' she greeted him. 'You know what they've done!' Hugo defended his friends: the fault was not theirs, but that of the management who had kept them shut up. She refused to be mollified.

'I've played before many audiences,' she said, 'but it's to you that I owe such an audience as this'.

Through a hole in the curtain, Hugo peered at the crowded auditorium. Amidst the rows of flowers and satins, of sober suits and greying pates, two blocks stood out distinctly, the hirsute and flamboyant ranks of *Jeunes-France*, their very appearance a provocation to the classicists. The 'gilet rouge' of Théophile Gautier—a deep pink satin doublet, worn with pale green trousers, black coat and wide-brimmed hat beneath which his rippling locks fell almost to his waist—was pointed at with especial horror; pale, impassive, he returned their stares with insolent sang-froid.

The three taps sounded. The curtain rose. In a lamp-lit sixteenth-century chamber the black-clad duenna hears the knock at the secret door of her mistress's outlawed lover:

[38]

Serait-ce déjà lui ? C'est bien à l'escalier
Dérobé— . . .

From the first lines the battle was engaged. With this audacious
enjambement (the carrying over of a phrase from one line to the next)
classical convention was deliberately scorned. From then on the evening was a tumult, 'barbarians' and classicists locked in deadly struggle.
'Brave times', wrote Théophile Gautier, 'when the things of the mind
and the intelligence could stir crowds to such excitement.' Hissed and
contested scene by scene and sometimes line by line, *Hernani* and the
romantics nonetheless carried the day. Only the most intransigent of
classicists could withstand the charm of Mademoiselle Mars in the final
act, in which Hernani, the outlaw chief, by then restored to his rightful
rank as Don Juan of Aragon, is about to celebrate his wedding to Dõna
Sol. 'Dressed in a gown of white satin,' wrote Madame Hugo, 'a crown
of white roses on her head, with her dazzling teeth and a figure which
was still that of an eighteen-year-old, she seemed a vision of youth and
beauty.'

The evening ended in an uproar of approval; only the classicists were
silent, not daring to hiss. Mademoiselle Mars, glowing, offered Hugo
her cheek to kiss. In Hugo's box, Madame Hugo, her head swathed in
a white scarf like a wimple (worn in fact because she was suffering from
toothache), acknowledged the cheers of her loyal battalions. Hugo took
no curtain calls, returning home *en bon bourgeois* to his apartment with a
little group of friends, carrying in his pocket, as concrete evidence of
his triumph, a publisher's contract for six thousand francs. It had come
in the nick of time—the family had been down to their last fifty.

Sainte-Beuve did not return with Hugo. He had gone to join his colleagues at the offices of the *Globe* where the editorial attitude towards
Hernani was being debated. The argument ranged back and forward,
anxiously followed by Sainte-Beuve, till a voice from the rear of the
room put an end to the discussion: 'Come on, Magnin [the reviewer],
plump for "admirable".'

The *Globe* came down wholeheartedly for Hugo and *Hernani*. 'This
great poetic composition', wrote Magnin, 'has succeeded beyond the
hopes and fears of friendship and of envy. Dazzled by so many beauties,
intoxicated by a poetry so alive and new, we will not hazard a judgement this evening: we will only announce the triumph of M. Victor
Hugo.'

The second and third nights of *Hernani* were as violently contested as
the first. 'From the literary hatreds which possess me', wrote Alfred de
Vigny who had loyally played his part in helping Hugo, 'I can understand the furies of 1793.' But the real confrontation came from the

[39]

fourth night onwards when Hugo's allocation of free tickets was reduced to only a hundred. His troops rose valiantly to the increased odds. Night after night they returned to the defence, making up in noise and ferocity for what they lacked in numbers. Not even the young and pretty were spared. A young woman, unwise enough to snigger at Hugo's verses, was sharply rebuked. 'Madame', she was told, 'you do wrong to laugh, you show your teeth.'

By the end of April, worn down by playing amidst continual uproar, the actors were exhausted, consoled however by the highest receipts for years. The play was taken off, after forty-nine performances. But the battle of *Hernani* had been won. Classical tradition lay in ruins; romantic drama held the stage and would do so for the next decade.

*   *   *

The tumultuous evenings at the Théâtre Français were still in full swing when on March 30th Victor Hugo, taking time off from his own theatrical battle, attended the first performance of Dumas' *Christine*.

Christine, it will be remembered, had first been accepted and then put aside by the Théâtre Français. Since then Dumas had become a famous figure. His love affairs were numerous, his wit and gaiety made him a star of literary salons. He himself knew the value of his effervescent personality. 'If I hadn't been there,' he remarked of a party he had attended, 'I might have found it rather boring.' His clothes bore witness to his new-found affluence: his waistcoats were magnificent, his watch-chain hung with jewels. 'How you negroes love trinkets,' Nodier teased him. His vanity was childlike and engaging. Sainte-Beuve described his talent as no more than 'a prodigious expenditure of animal spirits', but Dumas suffered from no doubts about his genius or his leading role in opening the way for romantic drama. A few years later, Hugo, meeting him, complained indignantly of a recent article in which Vigny had been described as the inventor of historical drama.

'Absurd,' agreed Dumas. 'As if everybody didn't know that it was I!'

Thanks to Dumas' new position and the changing public attitude, *Christine* was now well worth staging; he had accepted an offer to produce it from Charles-Jean Harel, director of the Odéon, whose mistress, Mademoiselle George, was eager to take the part of Christine.

Mademoiselle George reigned at the Odéon as Mademoiselle Mars did at the Théâtre Français. No two characters could have been more different off stage, Mademoiselle Mars ever conscious of her dignity, seldom allowing herself more than a thin-lipped smile, Mademoiselle George, despite her queenly appearance, ready to laugh wholeheartedly, receiving visitors without embarrassment in her bath. She had once been the mistress of Napoleon (though Stendhal calculated that she could not have slept with him more than sixteen times), and because of this and her Bonapartist sympathies could never hope to play at the Théâtre Français under Bourbon rule. She was forty-three, tall, statuesque, astonishingly beautiful despite a considerable *embonpoint*. 'How many fat queens and empresses', wrote Théophile Gautier, 'have been disinterred from history for her benefit!' The part of Christine might have been made for her.

The first performance of *Christine* had a mixed reception. The spirit of *Hernani* was abroad; classicists and romantics found a new battleground at the Odéon. But *Christine* was not *Hernani*, it was not even *Henri III*. The prose of *Henri III* had been vivid and swift; *Christine* was written in verse and Dumas was not a natural poet. Its greatest fault lay in its length. The performance went on for five hours, while the audience grew increasingly restive. When, in the course of a long-drawn epilogue, the queen asked her doctor:

'How much longer must I wait to die?'

a spectator called back:

'If you're not dead by one o'clock I'm going.'

When Dumas returned to his apartment where he had planned a party to celebrate, it was clear that his epilogue must be cut, that at least a hundred lines, which had been ill received, must be rewritten, and that, in order to be learnt and rehearsed by the next evening, the changes must be ready by morning. He had twenty-five guests to entertain. Hugo and Vigny, who were among them, told him to set his mind at rest, and while Dumas played his part as host they shut themselves up in a side-room to work on the play. When they had finished it was daybreak. Dumas' guests had all gone home or fallen asleep. Without waking anyone they laid the manuscript, corrected and ready for the theatre, on the chimney-piece, and went home arm in arm, like brothers.

*   *   *

In the Rue Notre-Dame-des-Champs the comings and goings of young men had proved too much for Hugo's landlady. One morning in April she called on Madame Hugo, now six months pregnant.

'My dear Madame,' she said, 'you are very nice and so is your husband, but you are not quiet enough for me. I retired from business in order to live in peace. I purposely bought this house in a street with no noise and for the last three months there has been an endless procession of people day and night, uproars on the staircase, earthquakes over my head . . . We can no longer live together.'

'You mean that you're giving us notice?'

'I'm truly sorry. You're a nice little family and you love your

[41]

children. But you don't get any sleep yourself. My poor dear, how I pity you. Your husband has chosen a hard profession . . .'

The Hugos were forced to move house, crossing the Seine to an apartment in the Rue Jean-Goujon, in the newly developing quarter of the Champs Elysées, still sparsely built up and surrounded by market gardens. Sainte-Beuve, already distraught and unhappy, was devastated by this separation. The daily visits which *Hernani* had so rudely interrupted could not be resumed. The journey from the Rue Notre-Dame-des-Champs was long and he could not be sure of finding them in when he got there. Once indeed the concierge turned him rudely away at the door. Hugo wrote to him the same day: 'We were there, dear friend. Imagine your annoyance! The concierges are stupid. Never listen to them and always come up.'

In the hope of regaining his spirits Sainte-Beuve left for Normandy to stay with his friend Ulric Guttinger. From there he wrote to Hugo: 'You are everything to me, my friend: I was nothing until I knew you and when I go away from you my flame is extinguished. It is truly dead. I have done nothing, thought of doing nothing, since my departure.'

Two months earlier his second volume of poetry, *Les Consolations*, had appeared. It had been dedicated to Hugo. 'My friend,' he wrote in the preface, 'this little book is yours; your name is on almost every page; your presence or your memory is mingled in all my thoughts.' The same melancholy, the same self-distrust and longing ran through it as had marked *Joseph Delorme*. In the earlier volume the Cénacle had brought meaning and inspiration to Joseph's wasted life; now it was in his friendship with the Hugos that Sainte-Beuve hoped to find salvation.

> Etres chers, objets purs de mon culte immortel
> Oh! dussiez-vous de loin, si mon destin m'entraîne,
> M'oublier, ou de près m'apercevoir à peine,
> Ailleurs, ici, toujours, vous serez tout pour moi!
> —Couple heureux et brillant, je ne vis plus qu'en toi.

Les Consolations marked the climax of Sainte-Beuve's friendship with the Hugos. He would look back on the six months in which they had been composed, the summer and autumn of 1829, as a 'celestial and fugitive' period of his life.

How fugitive was soon to appear. He returned from Normandy no happier than he had left. Hugo had written to him there, a letter full of affection: the *hernanistes* had gone, their new home felt empty without the presence of their friend, he was beginning to write poetry, he had written a poem for him and for Boulanger, both absent from Paris:

Amis, mes deux amis, mon peintre, mon poète!
Vous me manquez toujours, et mon âme inquiète
Vous redemande ici . . .

The assurances of friendship were unchanged, but to Sainte-Beuve it seemed that the feeling behind them had lost its former intensity. Hugo, immersed in literary creation, had less and less need of the subtle counsels of his friend; in his home, the kingdom of *marmots* (little children) over which he ruled, he enjoyed the emotional stability so pitifully lacking in Sainte-Beuve's own life. Sainte-Beuve returned from a visit to him more miserable than ever. 'My dear Victor,' he wrote, 'I wanted to write to you, for yesterday we were so sad, so cold, we left each other so unsatisfactorily that it caused me pain; I suffered from it all the evening on returning and all the night; I told myself it was impossible to see you often at this price, since I cannot see you always. What have we in fact to say to one another, to tell one another? Nothing, since we cannot share everything in common as before . . .'

And in another letter: 'My dear Victor, I am certain that you believe that I love you less, that someone other than you is replacing you in my affections; it's a superstition on my part, perhaps you have no such idea, you must forgive me. No, my dear friend, nothing has changed nor will change in me though I see you less than ever. If you only knew what I feel when I see you, when I return from your home and fall back again into my deathly solitude. Nothing, no one, not a living thing, and agonising memories of an intimacy I no longer possess . . .'

Paris had become unbearable for Sainte-Beuve. In early July he set off to Normandy to stay once more with Ulric Guttinger. He was still there when on July 26th the city, long simmering with discontent, broke into open revolution.

*   *   *

In May 1830, exasperated by the refusal of the liberal opposition—who held the majority—to pass the measures introduced by Polignac, the king had dissolved the Chambre des Députés and called an election, flinging all his personal prestige into an appeal to the electorate to support his official candidates. The result was a resounding defeat: the liberals were returned with a vastly increased majority, the king's party being outnumbered by nearly two to one. The conclusion was clear: Polignac must resign, the king must appoint a new chief minister acceptable to the majority.

The king had no such intention. It was by concessions, he declared, that his brother Louis XVI had met his fate. God had chosen him to rule: he would make no compromise. Moreover he felt his position to be strengthened by military victory, for in early July a French expedition launched against Algeria had ended in complete success. For the king the victory would prove Pyrrhic—when revolution came his best troops were in Algiers.

Armed with the news of the Algerian conquest, the king decided to stage a coup d'état. On July 25th, 'for the safety of the state', he issued the famous ordinances that would bring about his downfall: the dissolution of Parliament, the drastic reduction of the franchise, above all the suspension of the liberty of the press.

This last item sparked revolution. On July 26th while Charles, serenely self-assured, spent the day out hunting at Saint Cloud, a group of journalists, led by Thiers, issued a manifesto denouncing the ordinances as unconstitutional and calling on France to resist. On the 27th, the presses of the opposition papers, published in defiance of the ordinances, were destroyed by the police. Angry crowds began to gather. Factory- and shop-owners closed their premises, their workers spilled on to the streets, popular agitation was quickly fanned by the republicans. That evening, while garrison troops led by Marshal Marmont—a disastrous appointment since Marmont, who had deserted Napoleon, was a hated figure—moved into position on the boulevards, the barricades began to go up. Next morning the violence began, the insurgents—workers, students, printers, journalists—fighting beneath the tricolour, while the liberal bourgeoisie, true instigators of the revolt, stayed firmly behind closed doors. The weather was swelteringly hot. During the day the royalist troops, without food or water, battled through narrow twisting streets, assailed not only from the barricades but from the houses on either side. Confused and demoralised, uncertain of their loyalties, great numbers deserted to the other side. Anxious deputies, appalled by the turn of events, sent a deputation to Polignac who, as blindly confident as his master, refused to see them. By July 29th, after bitter fighting and the loss of more than two thousand lives, Paris was in the hands of the insurgents, the tricolour floated above the Tuileries, and the aged Talleyrand, watching the rout of Marmont's troops from his balcony, turned to dictate a note to his secretary: 'On the 29th of July, at precisely five minutes past twelve, the elder branch of the Bourbon family ceased to reign over France.'

But what of the younger branch? While the fighting raged in the streets of Paris, Charles X's cousin, the Duc d'Orléans, skulked in the suburbs, sending messages of loyalty to the king. Son of Philippe Egalité, who had signed the death warrant of Louis XVI, a soldier in the revolutionary army at Jemappes, he had all the qualifications necessary for a liberal monarch. It was to him that the deputies, alarmed by the popular fury that had been let loose and seeking to contain it, now turned. On July 30th, sweating with heat and nervousness, he was proclaimed 'Roi des Français' on the balcony of the Hôtel de Ville and, holding a tricolour in one hand, was publicly embraced by the hero of liberty, Lafayette. The crowd, persuaded by the tricolour, dispersed. The three days of revolution, 'Les Trois Glorieuses', were over.

The revolution, provoked by the king and fought by the people, had been won by the bourgeoisie. Louis-Philippe, the citizen king, came to power on a confidence trick. The young republicans who had fought his battles soon found their dreams of liberty betrayed; the power of the bourgeoisie was to replace that of the aristocracy and the slogan 'enrichissez-vous' express the ideals of the new governing class. As Charles X and his family rolled slowly in their coach to Cherbourg where a boat to England awaited them, the republican Pierre Leroux exclaimed: 'It must all be done over again. Let us relight the furnaces and cast new bullets.'

* * *

The romantics, united in their claim for liberty in the arts, had greeted political revolution in different ways. Dumas alone had played an active part. His exploits, recounted at length in his memoirs, included a daring dash to royalist Soissons to capture powder for the revolutionary forces.

Hector Berlioz had spent the three days shut up in the Institut de France where he was completing a fortnight's supervised confinement engaged in the musical competition which on this, his fourth attempt, would win him the Prix de Rome. He finished his work to the sound of gunfire, emerging on the evening of the 29th to join the triumphant rabble. 'I shall never forget how Paris looked during those famous days,' he wrote: 'the frantic bravery of the street-urchins, the enthusiasm of the men, the frenzied excitement of the whores, the grim resignation of the Swiss and Royal guards, the strange pride shown by the working class in being, as they said, the masters of Paris and stealing nothing; the incredible boasting of certain young men, who, having performed real feats of courage, contrived to make their exploits sound ridiculous with the fantastic embellishments they gave them in the telling.'

Alfred de Vigny was perhaps the only one of the romantics to retain a residual loyalty to Charles X. He had no illusions about his character or the folly of the ordinances but as a child at his father's knee he had kissed the cross of St Louis and he had served for thirteen thankless years as a soldier of the king. 'I have prepared my old uniform,' he wrote in his diary for the 28th. 'If the king calls for his officers I shall go . . . It is absurd. He will know neither my name nor what happens to me . . . And then to leave my mother and my young wife who depend on me! It is unjust; but I must do it.' But the king did not recall his officers, nor did he or the royal family leave the safety of Rambouillet. 'They do not come to Paris, where men are dying for them,' wrote Vigny. 'Race of Stuarts! Oh! I will stand by my own family.'

Hugo, the former panegyrist of royalty and the author of the official ode on the coronation of Charles X, also took no part in the events of 'Les Trois Glorieuses'. On the evening of the 28th, while the plain round the Champs Elysées filled up with troops, Adèle Hugo gave birth to a daughter 'amidst gunshots and cannonades'. Sainte-Beuve, on his return from Normandy, was asked to be the godfather, a role he accepted after hesitation, and only on the assurance that Madame Hugo herself desired it.

He had another role, no less important, to play in the immediate aftermath of the revolution—that of piloting Hugo through the 'still narrow straits of triumphant liberalism'. On August 9th Hugo's ode, 'A la Jeune France', celebrating the bravery of those who had fought to overthrow the crown, was published in the *Globe* with an introductory note, unsigned but written by Sainte-Beuve:

'Poetry has been swift to celebrate the grandeur of recent events . . . Here is M. Victor Hugo, who expresses in his turn, with a courage that is almost military, his patriotic devotion to a free and glorious France, his vivid sympathy for the youthful generation of which he is a brilliant leader; yet at the same time, by his early opinions, by the affections of his adolescence, to which he has consecrated more than one memorable ode, the poet is linked to the past which is finished and salutes it with a sad farewell even as he detaches himself from it.'

The political transition which had begun with the 'Ode à la Colonne' had been made. Sainte-Beuve's service to his friend, perhaps his last entirely disinterested one, had been to 'de-royalise' him.

*   *   *

During the fighting round the Champs Elysées Victor Hugo had moved his most precious effects to the house of his brother-in-law in a quarter well away from danger. Among them had been a notebook containing two months' worth of notes for his novel *Notre-Dame de Paris*, which had been lost in the haste of the removal. Hugo was already under pressure to complete his novel. His regular publisher, angered by his sale of *Hernani* to a rival, was holding him to a contract to complete it by December 1st, threatening to impose a penalty of a thousand francs for each week of delay thereafter. Hugo, still absorbed in his theatrical battles, had not yet begun to write it. A letter to the publisher, pleading the loss of the notebook and the exceptional circumstances that had occasioned it, gained him a temporary remission: the date of delivery was put back till February 1st 1831.

It was August. He had less than six months. Purchasing a bottle of ink and a long grey knitted garment which enveloped him from shoulder to toe, he locked away his clothes lest he should be tempted to go out, and shut himself up with his work, his only permitted distraction being an hour of conversation after dinner.

Adèle Hugo, tired and unwell after the birth of her child, was thrown back on her own resources. There was no longer the consolation of visits from the sympathetic Sainte-Beuve. Since his return to Paris he had avoided the Hugo ménage. 'Madame,' he wrote to Adèle in mid-September, 'I no longer see you or Victor. I am so full of my miserable affairs and unworthy of your peaceful conversation . . . But despite these apparent occupations and distractions there is emptiness and death in my heart. I beg you though to believe me when I tell you that the thought of you is always with me; do not imagine that I forget so long and sweet a friendship.'

Sainte-Beuve had returned to quarrels and dissension among the management of the *Globe*, politically divided after the events of July. In the course of a heated argument the editor had struck him across the face. A duel was arranged. On the morning of September 20th, in pouring rain, the two opponents faced each other in a wood outside Paris. Sainte-Beuve put up his umbrella despite protests that this was contrary to etiquette. 'I have no objection to being killed,' he said, 'but I do mind getting wet.' Fortunately the shots on both sides went wide. Honour was satisfied and the duelling party, according to Arsène Houssaye, ended with a picnic in the rain.

Madame Hugo, hearing of the incident after it was over, wrote to Sainte-Beuve expressing her disquiet at the danger he had run and scolding him gently, on behalf of her husband and herself, for not coming to see his old friends.

But Sainte-Beuve was far past gentle scoldings. Lonely, impoverished, jealous of the success which had made Hugo a public figure, he could no longer hide a deeper feeling, his jealousy of the husband of Adèle. It was during that 'celestial' summer of 1829, the summer of *Les Consolations*, that he had fallen in love. A poem from his *Livre d'Amour**

---

* *Le Livre d'Amour*, a collection of poems written from 1831 to 1837, traced the course of Sainte-Beuve's relationship with Adèle Hugo. He considered them his finest work and in 1843, literary vanity overriding discretion, for both Adèle and her husband were clearly recognisable in the poems, he had them privately printed and circulated copies among his closest friends. Scandal broke out two years later when the editor of a scurrilous magazine, *Les Guêpes*, who had been shown the proofs of *Le Livre d'Amour* by a compositor in the printing works where they had been set up,

recaptures the moment when friendship first became coloured with desire. She was before a mirror, adjusting her heavy black hair, which had become unknotted and was tumbling down about her shoulders:

> J'allais sortir alors, mais tu me dis: 'Restez!'
> Et, sous tes doigts pleuvant, la chevelure immense
> Exhalait jusqu'à moi les odeurs de la semence . . .

An explanation with Hugo had become inevitable. Some time, either in late November or early December, a meeting took place, during which Sainte-Beuve appears to have confessed his love and Hugo, preferring magnanimity to the role of a jealous husband—and moreover totally confident of his wife's fidelity—reacted with generosity and affection, assuring Sainte-Beuve of his friendship and begging him to overcome his feelings and to continue his relationship with them as before. Sainte-Beuve, shamed and humiliated, had no reply.

Hugo's trust in his wife was unshaken, but his domestic happiness was already clouded. Since the birth of their baby Adèle, exhausted by child-bearing—five children in eight years—had refused to have further physical relations with him. Hugo had been a virgin when he had married her at twenty; ardent and passionate, he had lived for eight years in the illusion of a perfect marriage. But Adèle, often tearful, was plainly far from sharing it.

Sainte-Beuve, despite their interview, did not let matters rest. On December 7th he wrote Hugo a despairing letter:

'I can no longer bear it; if you knew how my days and nights are passed and what contradictory passions I am prey to, you would have pity on the man who has offended you . . . There is despair in my heart and rage; a desire to kill you, to assassinate you. Forgive me these horrible feelings—but think of this, you whose mind is so thronged with thoughts, think of the void which so great a friendship leaves. What? Lost for ever? I can no longer come to see you, I shall never again set foot on your threshold—it is impossible . . . What would I be doing now by your fireside, now that I have deserved your mistrust, when suspicion glides between us, when your surveillance is uneasy, when Madame Hugo cannot even catch my glance without having first consulted yours? . . . You had the generosity to beg me to come freely as in the past, but it was compassion and indulgence on your part for a

---

published an article denouncing the author under the heading of 'An Infamy'. Hugo made no public comment, expressing his anger only in a vitriolic sonnet which was not published till seven years after his death.

weakness which you thought such a gesture could console. I cannot consent to it; it would be too great a torture for me . . .'

Hugo, despite the urgent pressure of his work, wrote back immediately, with patience and affection:

'. . . Let us be indulgent towards one another, my friend. I have my wound, you have yours; the painful shock will pass. Time heals everything; let us hope that one day we will find in all this only one more reason to love one another better. My wife has read your letter. Come and see me often. Write to me always . . .'

Sainte-Beuve's next letter, written a fortnight later, was couched in a calmer tone. To see Hugo would be unbearable, but he would write, if only to prove that there was in his heart 'a light which burns and a thought which prays eternally at the tomb of our friendship'.

'You did well to write to me, my friend, you did well for all of us,' Hugo replied. 'We read your letters together, my wife and I, and we speak of you with deepest affection. The times that you recall are full of happiness. Do you imagine that they will never come again? As for me, I hope they will. There will always be joy for me in seeing you, in writing to you. There are only one or two realities in life and friendship is one of them. Let us write to one another, let us write often. Our hearts will continue to speak to one another. Nothing is broken between us . . .'

On this note the year ended, Hugo generous and consoling, Sainte-Beuve stricken with remorse, both roles becoming ones. But what were the thoughts of Adèle, the passive Adèle, that 'enigma', wrote Sainte-Beuve, 'of sensibility and profundity'? Her role in the triangle had not yet been defined.

[5]

1831

On January 1st Sainte-Beuve sent new year presents to Hugo's children. Little Léopoldine, aged six and a half, wrote to thank him and with her letter came a note from Hugo:

'You've been very kind to my little ones, my friend. We'd like to thank you, my wife and I. Come and dine with us on Tuesday, the day after tomorrow. *1830 is over.*'

On the 14th Hugo finished his *Notre-Dame de Paris* and with it the bottle of ink which he had brought to begin it. He had arrived at the last drop and the last line at the same instant—which gave him, for a moment, the idea of changing the title of the book to *Ce qu'il y a dans une bouteille d'encre*, a title he later offered to the novelist Alphonse Karr. Hugo, who had sat down to write with a heavy heart, now left his characters and the prodigious cathedral which overshadowed them, with as much reluctance as he had begun work.

The book was published in March. Its success was immediate and immense: Claude Frollo, the archdeacon, the hideous Quasimodo, the gipsy Esmeralda, all passed into the popular imagination where they have remained ever since. His novel, wrote Hugo to his publisher, 'had no historical pretensions save to depict, perhaps with a certain scholarship and science, but only by insights and glimpses, the state of morals, beliefs, laws, arts, of civilisation in fact, in the fifteenth century. For the rest, it is not that which matters in a book. If it has any merit it is as a work of imagination, of fantasy and caprice.'

Sainte-Beuve would not write a review of *Notre-Dame de Paris*, which it was not in his nature to admire. His earliest reservations about Hugo's work, his distrust of imaginative excess, expressed in his review of *Odes et Ballades*, had only deepened with time. A classicist in his sense of measure, he preferred, in Arsène Houssaye's phrase, to reign on the moderate slopes of literature. Moreover, for political as well as literary reasons his enchantment with romanticism was beginning to wane. The poet of the Cénacle, the enraptured herald of the romantic movement, could now write in an article: 'Unhappily the romantic association, formulated under the Restoration, was too restricted in itself, not closely enough involved in the profound movements of society; the Cénacle was, after all, no more than a salon . . .'

And indeed the Cénacle was dissolving fast. Vigny already stood aloof; Mérimée was sarcastic and withdrawn; Théophile Gautier, Gérard de Nerval and the younger *chevaliers d'Hernani* formed a group apart, living a merrily bohemian life in garret rooms adorned with skulls and the paintings of their friends; Dumas was absorbed in love affairs and theatrical successes.

Alfred de Musset too, the 'spoilt child' of the Cénacle, was 'de-hugotising' himself. His first poems, *Contes d'Espagne et d'Italie,* had been touched by the rays of *Les Orientales,* but he did not stay long under the influence of the romantic leader. Nor did he make the mistake of confusing creation with literary friendships. In a letter to his brother that summer, he wrote:

'I met Eugène Delacroix one evening, coming back from the theatre; we talked painting in the street from his door to mine, from my door to his, until two in the morning; we couldn't leave off. With good old Antony Deschamps I've talked on the boulevard, from eight to eleven in the evening. When I leave Nodier or Achille [Devéria] I argue up and down the street with one or the other. Will any of us write a better poem or paint a better picture as a result? Each of us has within him a single note which only he can sound . . . All the reasoning in the world cannot make the song of a blackbird emerge from the throat of a starling. What is necessary to the artist, as to the poet, is emotion. When I feel, in writing a poem, a certain beating of the heart which I recognise, then I know that my verses are the best that I can do.'

The world of the Cénacle, in any case, was only part of Musset's life. He was young, he was charming, he was well born: he flung himself with avidity into the role of fashionable dandy, spending a fortune, which he did not possess, at the tailor's, falling in love 'as other people catch a cold', drinking and gambling through the night. 'Make no mistake,' said a friend to his brother, who had been watching Musset at a ball, 'your brother is destined to be a great poet; but when I see his face light up at the pleasures of this world, his air of an escaped colt, the way he looks at women and the way they look at him, I fear his meeting with Delilahs.'

Social gaieties went with more dubious pleasures. So, for instance, we hear of him in a letter from Mérimée: 'Musset, who had been all affectation till the champagne came, finding himself drunk at dessert, became natural and amusing. He proposed to give us an exhibition of himself making love to a girl by the light of twenty-five candles. The proposition being accepted with alacrity, we went straight away to put it into execution . . . Arrived at our destination however, our romantic poet developed a nose-bleed and began all sorts of "ifs" and "buts". In brief, despite all our efforts and the science of two quite pretty girls, we could get no results . . .'

[51]

After the success of his *Contes d'Espagne et d'Italie*, which had won him immediate fame, Musset had met with total failure with his next work, his play *La Nuit Vénitienne*. It was presented at the Odéon in December 1830: witty, light and charming, it was too delicate a piece for a theatre so vast and imposing and for the rowdiness of a post-revolutionary audience. Worse, the first night was bedevilled by a ludicrous accident. During the love scene in the second act the heroine Laurette, a ravishing figure in white satin, leant back against a painted trellis; the paint, alas, had not dried and when she turned her back to the audience her dress was seen to be barred with green. It was enough to overthrow the play, which was hissed to the end. Musset was deeply mortified. 'I would never have believed that Paris could provide so stupid an audience,' he exclaimed at the height of the uproar, and after a second evening which, despite the removal of the fatal trellis, was no more successful than the first, he withdrew the play. 'I have done with the menagerie,' he wrote of the theatrical public, 'and that for a long time.'*

Disillusioned by his experience, Musset wrote little during 1831, but he read much, thought much and, according to his brother, perhaps lived more fully than was necessary for a poet. One evening in October he found him alone with his head in his hands.

'I'm thinking,' Musset said, 'that in two months I shall be twenty-one and that is a great age. Do I really need to see so many men and listen to so many women talk in order to know them? Haven't I seen enough to have plenty to say, if I'm capable of saying anything? Either there is nothing within me and then sensations will awaken nothing in my spirit, or else I bear within myself the elements of everything, and need only see a little to guess at all. Nevertheless I feel that something is still lacking. Is it a great love? Is it a great sorrow? Perhaps both . . .'

*   *   *

The failure of *La Nuit Vénitienne* left Hugo, Dumas and Vigny as the uncontested triumvirate of the romantic stage. Each one moved on to new successes in 1831. Vigny alone had not yet produced an original work. His *Othello*, freely translated and rising to great poetic heights, was nonetheless an adaptation. Some inhibition seemed to have kept him from giving himself entirely to the stage. With his usual habit of self-examination he had analysed this unease. 'I have long sought the cause of the secret antipathy which has kept me from writing for the theatre,' he wrote in his diary, 'an antipathy especially strange in me

* He did not have another play performed in public until 1847.

whose chief talent or instinct lies in dramatic composition.' It was due, he concluded, to the fact that in drama the interpretation, and hence the chief source of emotion, must always remain outside the author's control.

One actress would break down this inhibition and it was with her as his inspiration that Vigny, in the summer of 1830, had written his first dramatic work, *La Maréchale d'Ancre*. 'I wrote it for Marie Dorval', he confided in his diary, and it was in the house of her husband, the dramatic critic Toussaint Merle, that he gave a reading of the play in November 1830.

In the event Marie Dorval was unable to take the part. She was already committed to another seventeenth-century role, that of Hugo's Marion de Lorme. Vigny's play, set in the same period, was too close in subject matter to appear at the same theatre and with the same actress. Moreover the formidable Mademoiselle George, with the power of the Odéon behind her, had set her heart on playing the role herself. Marie Dorval, who attended the first night, must have felt a certain satisfaction when at the end of the second act the statuesque Mademoiselle George, 'gravely indisposed', was compelled to abandon the performance—her indisposition, murmured unkind spirits, was due to the fact that her corsets were too tightly laced. The following night, however, with Mademoiselle George recovered and resplendent in red velvet, won Vigny an honourable success.

If Mademoiselle George and Mademoiselle Mars saw themselves as queens of their respective theatres, Marie Dorval had no such pretensions. The darling of the boulevards, she was unashamedly plebeian. Her hoarse, breathless voice could switch in a moment from tender emotion to wild laughter or fishwife's abuse. Her large, melancholy eyes could sparkle with gaiety or convey an unbearable pathos. She responded intuitively to her roles: rejecting and indeed incapable of the majesty of classical theatre, she carried naturalism to the point of frenzied self-abandon. Frail, dark-skinned, with irregular features and a high rounded forehead, she was 'better than pretty, she was charming,' wrote George Sand; 'and yet she was pretty but so charming that it was unnecessary.'

The daughter of strolling players, she had passed a miserable childhood trailing round the theatres of the provinces, playing in one-night stands almost as soon as she could walk. Orphaned at fifteen, she had married a fellow actor who died soon after, leaving her with two small children to support; a third child was born a few years later after a liaison with the conductor Piccini. After many hardships and vicissitudes she had reached Paris and the Porte-Saint-Martin theatre, home of vaudeville and melodrama, and it was there, in 1827, that she had her first great triumph, playing opposite Frédérick Lemaître in *Trente Ans dans la Vie d'un Joueur*. With Lemaître she now dominated the popular stage, bringing to melodrama that quality of lyricism which, in the words of Charles Nodier, was the essence of romantic theatre. 'I regard her', wrote Alfred de Vigny in his diary, 'as the greatest tragédienne alive today.' Night after night, leaving his wife at home, he would go to watch her at the Porte-Saint-Martin. Before he met her she was already a vision and an ideal, 'une beauté', he wrote,

> Qui toujours passe en pleurs parmi d'autre figures
> Comme un pâle rayon dans les forêts obscures,
> Triste, simple et terrible . . .

* * *

Vigny had first met Marie Dorval in 1830. He had come to join Musset and Dumas at the Café des Variétés. Musset was not there but Dumas was sitting at a table with Marie Dorval. After introducing her to Vigny he got up to greet some other friends, leaving the two of them alone together.

Some time later—in the spring of 1831—Dumas called on Marie Dorval, carrying the manuscript of a play. He was surprised at the formality of her greeting.

'Is this the way you kiss old friends?'

'I can't kiss you any other way . . . I'm like Marion de Lorme; I've taken up virginity again.'

'Impossible!'

'On my word of honour! I'm becoming virtuous.'

'And who the devil has brought this about?'

'Alfred de Vigny.'

'You love him?'

'More than I can say; I'm crazy about him . . .'

Dumas saw that Marie Dorval was in earnest. 'There are certain men,' she told him, 'that one does not deceive; they are men of genius; or if one does so, so much the worse for the deceiver. All the same,' she added, 'it may not last for ever . . . If I ever change my mind I will write to you.'

'To me?'

'Yes, to you.'

'Before anyone else?'

'Before anyone else. You know how fond I am of you, *mon bon chien*.'

And on this friendly understanding she turned to the manuscript which Dumas had brought with him. It was that of his play *Antony*. Marie Dorval leant over his shoulder as he read it to her. Her heart beat faster against him, he wrote, when he reached the end of the second act, and her tears began to drop on the paper.

For *Antony* was a drama of emotion. Based on Dumas' own love affair with a married woman, its theme was adultery, its hero a bastard, an outcast from a society whose hypocrisy and injustice he condemns. The first romantic drama with a modern setting, it matched the sixteenth and seventeenth centuries in the violence of its passions and its sensational dénouement, described by Dumas in his memoirs: 'A man, surprised by the husband of his mistress, kills her, declaring that she was resisting him, and for this murder he dies on the scaffold. Thus he both saves the honour of the woman and expiates his crime.'

The play had been destined for the Théâtre Français, but from the first rehearsals it became clear that the parts of Adèle Hervey, the erring wife, and of Antony, the moody, Byronic and embittered hero, were beyond the emotional range of Mademoiselle Mars and her partner Firmin. Neither was cast in a suitably 'fatal' mould, neither had that romantic pallor so essential to the roles. Mademoiselle Mars, said Dumas, dared not, Firmin could not, be pale.

When four days before the opening, after numberless delays and provocations, Mademoiselle Mars announced her intention of postponing her performance for a further three months, Dumas' much tried patience broke.

'There is only one objection to your plan, Madame,' he said.

'And what is that?'

'In three months' time my piece will already have been played.'

'What do you mean, already played?'

'What I say.'

'And where, may I ask?'

'At the Porte-Saint-Martin theatre.'

And, picking up the manuscript of his play, he had set off for the house of Marie Dorval.

Marie Dorval was delighted to take a part which had been withdrawn from Mademoiselle Mars, a part too in which for the first time she would play a *femme du monde*. Only the last act, which Dumas had toned down to suit Mademoiselle Mars, left her dissatisfied. She insisted on his re-writing it, installing him that very night at a desk in her absent husband's room. By dawn Dumas had completed his task and the play was ready to be taken to the director of the Porte-Saint-Martin. Marie Dorval clapped her hands with enthusiasm. 'Just wait till you hear how I'll say "Mais je suis perdue, moi!" and then, "Ma fille! Il faut que j'embrasse ma fille", and then "Tue moi!"—just wait!'

[55]

The first night of *Antony* was a success to rival *Hernani*. For the first time an audience drawn from society and the salons flocked to this theatre of the boulevards, the young women with leg-of-mutton sleeves and hair *à la giraffe* in the fashion of the day, the young men with extravagant waistcoats and velvet-trimmed jackets. From time to time the crowd on the pavement would part to let some celebrity pass, a poet or a painter, for the Cénacle was there in force that evening.

The part of Antony was played by Pierre Bocage, a 'fatal' man *par excellence*, melancholy, sarcastic, given to violent accesses of passion, his air of mystery veiling the gaps in Dumas' characterisation. Marie Dorval, in a muslin town dress, did not please at first: the part of a lady of fashion was unfamiliar to her, her voice was too hoarse, her gestures too emphatic. But as the plot gathered momentum she swept the audience with her. 'The burning passion of the play set every heart alight,' wrote Théophile Gautier. 'The young women were mad with love for Antony; the young men would have blown out their brains for Adèle.' Dumas, a true man of the theatre, knowing that the momentum of the play would be lost if the intervals were too long, hastened the changing of the scenes so that between the fourth act and the fifth the applause had not died down before the curtain was raised once more. The last act, the one which Dumas had re-written for Dorval, ended with the famous finale. Adèle Hervey, discovered by her husband, begs her lover Antony to kill her. He stabs her after a final kiss, and as her husband rushes in confronts him over her dead body:

'Elle me résistait. Je l'ai assassinée.'

The audience were beside themselves. Dumas was mobbed by an admiring crowd, his green coat torn apart and the shreds treasured as relics by his devotees.

As for the famous dénouement, it became part of popular mythology; the humblest Parisian, who had never seen or read the play, could quote the final lines. Some years later, at a repeat performance, with the same two actors, a careless stage manager rang down the curtain too soon. The audience, baulked of their finale, threatened to break up the benches. Bocage, furious at the ruin of his effect, remained sulking in his dressing-room and refused to return to the stage. It was left to Dorval to put matters right. The curtain was raised again. Getting up from the sofa on which she had lain as dead, she advanced to the footlights.

'Messieurs,' she cried, 'je lui résistais; il m'a assassinée!'

*   *   *

The influence of *Antony* rippled through society. The youthful generation, who saw their passions reflected in the play, took Antony

[56]

for their model. 'A damned soul lurked beneath every suit and waist-coat *à la Vénitienne*', wrote Louis Maigron in *Le Romantisme et les Moeurs*. 'Everywhere you met with desperate attitudes, sombre glances, fatal brows, mocking laughter, convulsive sobs, fists raised to heaven, blasphemies and maledictions. Women abandoned themselves, thrilling —since everything is possible—with the hope of reclaiming these accursed ones.' As for husbands, that long-suffering group, never had their role been harder. 'If trade unions had been invented at that time, there is no doubt that husbands might have formed one—and it would have been a powerful body—against the personal enemies of their happiness, the romantics.'

Dumas himself, so robust and cheerful, made a poor attempt to assume the Byronic gloom of his hero:

> Malheur, malheur à moi, que le ciel, en ce monde
> A jeté comme un hôte à ses lois étranger!
> A moi qui ne sais pas, dans ma douleur profonde,
> Souffrir longtemps sans me venger.

But the stormy love affair which had given rise to his play had died down long before the first night. From a box Mélanie Waldor, his discarded mistress, listened to the love scenes she had inspired and returned home alone in tears. However, since she was a literary hostess as well as a romantic heroine, she did not break entirely with her former lover, whose celebrity brought lustre to her salon.

Dumas' new love was an actress, Belle Krelshamer, a black-haired beauty with azure eyes, by whom in March he had had a daughter. Unwilling to marry the mother, he agreed to recognise the child legally, giving her the surname Dumas. Having done so, and having in the personage of Antony taken on the defence of bastards, his thoughts turned naturally to his other son, the seven-year-old Alexandre, whose paternity he had never officially recognised and whose legal guardianship he now assumed.

The boy was living with his mother, Catherine Lebay, in the pretty suburb of Passy where Dumas, after the success of *Henri III*, had installed them in a small apartment. Catherine Lebay, aware that Dumas' generosity came in fits and starts, had started a small dress-making business, living frugally in order to support the son whom she adored and who adored her. Their happiness was now abruptly broken. Dumas, pushed by Belle Krelshamer, who represented Catherine Lebay as vulgar and uneducated, made up his mind—no doubt with good intentions, for he loved the child—to take over his upbringing himself. In vain Catherine attempted a lawsuit, in vain, frantic with grief, she tried to hide the child under the bed when the authorities called; as an unmarried mother she had no legal rights. The law was inexorable. Alexandre was taken from his mother, to be sent by his father to a boarding school. All his life he would remember his last evening before parting from her: the silver set of cutlery she had bought for him, the little toys, the clothes laid out with care. 'Each object represented a sum of money painfully acquired, work prolonged into the night, sometimes until morning.' And when the door of the boarding school shut behind him the next day he followed her in imagination down the street. 'I could see her, her handkerchief to her eyes to hide her tears from strangers, walking home with a rapid step, and once there abandoning herself to her emotion, then drying her eyes with that courage of which I had seen so many proofs, returning to her daily work, replying amiably to the questions which the seamstresses were bound to ask her.'

The pain of that separation would never wholly leave him.

*   *   *

On August 11th Hugo's *Marion de Lorme*, re-instated by the censor, opened at the Porte-Saint-Martin. Thanks to Hugo's fame and literary prestige the theatre could at last be said to have arrived. Marie Dorval, speaking in alexandrines, at one moment even quoting from Corneille, was able to show herself the equal of Mars and George. No wonder that when Hugo had brought her the play she had flung her arms round his neck, declaring that she had never had so marvellous a part. 'Drama had taken her from melodrama,' wrote Gautier, 'poetry had won her from the slang of the boulevards. How she glowed with happiness and pride; how completely at ease she seemed with that tremendous passion and tremendous style; how effortlessly she soared, borne by the powerful breath of the young master. We can see her still, with her satin dress, her long hair twisted with pearls . . .'

Despite Dorval, despite the magnificence of the poetry which clothed this story of a courtesan redeemed by love, *Marion de Lorme* was no more than a half-success. Political excitements had succeeded those of *Hernani*; the ardour of the young romantic battalions had been largely dissipated; there was no enthusiastic claque to carry it through. Behind scenes too there was confusion: the director was absent, there were rumours that he was planning to sell the theatre. And, in fact, on the very day before the first night came the news that Harel, the director of the Odéon, urged by the ambitious Mademoiselle George, had bought the licence of the Porte-Saint-Martin for an enormous sum. Dorval met Hugo in a fury. 'It's inconceivable that anyone could be such an imbecile as to sell the theatre the day before a new production . . . it's we who'll pay for it in fallen receipts.'

'Madame,' said Hugo, 'your anger gives you new verve; you will give a wonderful performance.'

But Dorval refused to be calmed by compliments and continued to abuse the director in language too vigorous, according to Adèle Hugo, to reproduce in print.

The takings for *Marion de Lorme*, as Dorval had predicted, were far below those of *Hernani*. Hugo, the careful householder, supervised them anxiously. 'Hugo is terrible with his preoccupation with receipts,' wrote the young poet Antoine Fontaney. And on another evening: 'We are going to see Madame Dorval who is, they say, not well. Thus the receipts are held up; it is a great worry. Oh, receipts! Receipts!'

1831 was a year of masterpieces for Hugo: in the spring his *Notre-Dame de Paris*, that summer *Marion de Lorme*, in the autumn his collection of poems *Les Feuilles d'Automne*. Any one of these would have been enough to assure his fame. At twenty-nine, with Lamartine and Châteaubriand temporarily silent, he could be considered the greatest writer in France, perhaps in Europe.

And yet it was a year of desolation for him too. The wound which Sainte-Beuve had opened refused to heal. In March and April there had been a patched up sort of reconciliation. Sainte-Beuve returned on his ancient footing as an habitué of the house, but things were no longer the same. He felt he had been humiliated before Adèle; to win her, in the face of her husband's noble attitudes, would restore his self-respect. Adèle, her *amour-propre* long bruised by Hugo's absorption in his work, was not insensible to Sainte-Beuve's devotion, so flattering and so undemanding. Hugo could not hide his uneasiness at seeing them both together; to appease him Adèle begged him always to be present when Sainte-Beuve called. All the same, she was seeing Sainte-Beuve in secret—in parks, in shadowy corners of churches—calming any feelings of guilt with the thought that their relations were wholly innocent.

Imperceptibly her affections were slipping away from her husband. Hugo could feel this, though he was only confusedly aware of the reason. He assailed her with scenes, she wept, he begged her forgiveness. Only the news that Sainte-Beuve was soon to go away, to take up a professorship in Belgium, reconciled him to a situation which he was finding insupportable.

Then, in July, perhaps at Adèle's instigation, Sainte-Beuve announced his decision to remain in Paris. Hugo could bear it no longer.

'What I have to say, my friend,' he wrote, 'causes me profound pain, but I must say it. Your departure for Liège would have spared me and it was for that reason that I must have seemed to you to wish for something which, at any other time, would have been a real unhappiness for me, your departure . . .

'I do not know if you reached, as I have, the bitter conclusion that this attempt at three months of half-intimacy, ill begun and ill continued, has failed. When you are not there I feel in the depths of my heart that I love you as before; when you are there it is a torture . . .

'Let us then cease to see one another for a time, dear friend, in order not to cease to love one another . . . The distance between our homes, the summer, visits to the country, the fact that I'm never at home, are pretexts enough for the outside world. As for ourselves we will know what to think. We will always love one another. We will write, will we not? . . .'

Feigning surprise, Sainte-Beuve wrote back, assuring Hugo of his loyalty and accepting with resignation but regret his decision not to see him.

To which the trusting Hugo: 'I have received your letter, my dear friend, and it rends my heart. You are right in everything, your conduct has been loyal and perfect . . . Everything is in my poor unhappy head, my friend. I love you at this moment more than ever and, without exaggeration, I hate myself, I hate myself for being mad and ill to this point. The day that you wish me to offer my life for your sake, you may have it, it is no great sacrifice. For you see, and I say it to you *alone*, I am no longer happy. I have acquired the conviction that it is possible that she whom I love no longer loves me, and that it is perhaps in part because of you. In vain I repeat to myself everything that you say to me, and that the very thought is madness, there is always this drop of poison which is enough to infect my whole life. Have pity on me; I am truly unhappy. I no longer know where I am with the two beings I love most in the world. You are one of them . . .'

Sainte-Beuve could not but respond, or appear to respond, to Hugo's plea for pity. He busied himself on his behalf on the literary plane. He had not reviewed *Notre-Dame de Paris*; he made up for it with an eulogistic biography of Hugo in the *Revue des Deux Mondes*, with support for *Marion de Lorme*, and in December with an article on *Les Feuilles d'Automne* in which awe and admiration for Hugo as a poet transcended all personal pettiness.

But in private he was free with allusions to his love—in contrast to Hugo who, schooled by experience as the child of separated parents, spoke of his unhappiness to no one but the man who had caused it. Sainte-Beuve had no such reserves, even with slight acquaintances. Thus Fontaney, in his diary of October 1st, writes of a conversation with Sainte-Beuve: 'We spoke of Victor. "He is a wretch," he told me. And he made me the strangest confidences. Victor has become jealous!

And out of arrogance! And that is the reason for his wife's illness! He says there is no feeling in the depths of Hugo's soul, only granite and iron! And he, poor Sainte-Beuve, loved and took himself away. There were explanations, letters, there was an arranged absence; to distract himself Sainte-Beuve took up politics and Saint Simonism; then he was summoned back, then banished again for ever. Adèle is locked up and they no longer see one another.'

Adèle indeed was not well—since the birth of her child she had been suffering with pains in her back—but she was certainly not shut up at home. On the contrary she was continuing to see Sainte-Beuve. He was writing poetry for her in which Hugo, 'le jaloux', featured as a tyrant and Adèle as the tender victim of his passion:

> Adèle! tendre agneau! que de luttes dans l'ombre
> Quand ton lion jaloux, hors de lui, la voix sombre
> Revenant, usurpant sa place à ton côté,
> Demandant son droit, sa part dans ta beauté,
> Et qu'en ses bras de fer, brisée, évanouie,
> Tu retrouveras toujours quelque ruse inouïe
> Pour te garder fidèle au timide vainqueur
> Qui ne veut et n'aura de toi que ton coeur . . .

Hugo, that autumn, was seen by his friends to be agitated and unhappy. He spoke of going away for a year alone, of a voyage to Egypt, to Italy, to Spain. He could no longer conceal from himself, even if rumour to that effect did not reach him, that his wife was not in love with him. 'Woe to him who loves and is not loved,' he wrote years later. '. . . Consider this woman. She is charming. She is gentle, white and guileless. She is the joy and love of your home. But she does not love you. She does not hate you either. She does not love you, that is all. Fathom, if you dare, the depths of such despair. Look at her; she does not understand you. Speak to her; she does not hear. All your thoughts of love are centred on her; she lets them go as they have come, neither entertaining nor rejecting them. The rock in the midst of the ocean is not more indifferent, impassive, immutable, than the insensibility in her heart. You love her. Alas! You are lost . . .'

6

1832

The year began under sinister auspices. An epidemic of cholera, which had swept through Russia and northern Europe in the previous year, had broken out in England. It could only be a matter of time before it crossed to France.

In the shadow of the plague Paris waited in a restless mood. The year that followed the July revolution had been punctuated by riots and disturbances from both the left and the right. The king's claim to rule was based neither on the principle of legitimacy nor that of democratic choice; he trod an uneasy path between the two extremes of opposition. But behind the façade of a perfect bourgeois, he concealed the will of a Bourbon, a limitless capacity for intrigue, and an instinct for survival that had seen him through many vicissitudes. Unpretentious and approachable in his manner, he consciously courted popularity. Alfred de Vigny pictures him in his journal as he pushed his way, affably and without ceremony, through a Paris crowd:

'I saw a multitude of men, women and children in the midst of whom, struggling to pass through, was a man in a grey hat and brown suit, with a large umbrella under his arm, giving handshakes on all sides to whoever happened to be nearest . . . arriving at the great staircase in a dishevelled state, his waistcoat unbuttoned, his cuffs torn and his hat crushed by the greetings he had been giving to the throng that had swamped him: it was the king.'

On March 26th, in the midst of carnival celebrations for the *mi-carême* or mid-Lent festivities, the first case of cholera was reported in Paris. The news, wrote Dumas, came like some biblical malediction. People fled to their houses in terror, leaving the streets deserted, shutting their doors and windows against the invisible assassin. Within a week the number of dead had reached the hundreds. In the poorer quarters there were riots among the working classes, who were convinced that the authorities were trying to poison them, and a number of luckless shopkeepers, suspected of abetting them, were lynched or torn to pieces. By mid-April the plague had reached its crisis point, with more than a thousand deaths recorded a day.

Alfred de Musset's father, amiable, cultivated, indulgent to his wayward son, was one of the early victims. Musset's grief was silent and profound. It was one of those sorrows, he told his brother, 'that tears can never soften and whose memory will always retain its first bitterness and horror'. His father's death, and the loss of his salary as a civil servant, left the family's financial future uncertain. Musset faced his responsibilities. Rather than be a burden to the mother and sister he adored, he would make one final attempt in the literary field, and if a second volume of poems failed he would enlist in a cavalry regiment. 'The uniform will suit me well,' he said. He set to work, taking as his theme an oriental proverb sadly apposite to his own experience: 'Between the cup and the lip there is always room for sorrow.'

The cholera continued through the spring and early summer. Fontaney, in his journal for those months, describes the empty streets where hearses stood in ranks like cabs; the cemeteries where huge communal trenches were dug to receive the dead, and where old coffins, their contents only half-rotted, were broken up to make way for new; the blue skies and bright spring sunshine that seemed to mock the sufferings of the stricken city. Typically romantic in his morbid curiosity, he went with Mérimée to the Hôtel-Dieu to see the patients in the wards, descending afterwards to the cellar of the hospital where the dead, wrapped in white sheets, were laid out like so many mummies. Later that day he attended a gathering at Victor Hugo's flat, where Liszt was seated at the piano. He played a funeral march by Beethoven. 'It was magnificent,' wrote Fontaney. 'What a wonderful scene you could set to it. The dead from cholera marching to Notre-Dame in their shrouds!'

Not long afterwards cholera struck Hugo's own family. His five-year-old son Charles Victor, 'dear little fat Charlot', was sent home from school with suspected food poisoning. Before long he was seized with the terrible thirst that was a symptom of the disease; his body became rigid and cold and his fingernails turned black.

Hugo had already known the anguish of losing a child, his first-born son, three months old. He would allow no one else to look after Charlot, spending the entire night rubbing his body with warmed flannels, on the doctor's orders, to restore his circulation. Hugo loved his children passionately.

Je ne veux habiter la cité des vivants,

he wrote in *Les Feuilles d'Automne*,

Que dans une maison qu'une rumeur d'enfants
Fasse toujours vivante et folle.

Next morning, thanks perhaps to his father's care, the child showed signs of returning warmth and colour. Within three days he had recovered. 'Charlot's cholera, which was genuine, has been much exaggerated,' wrote Sainte-Beuve to Victor Pavie. Unable to call on the Hugos, he had sent round anxious enquiries.

Throughout the epidemic the theatres stood half-empty. While Alfred de Vigny, stricken himself, lay close to death, Marie Dorval was playing at the Porte-Saint-Martin in a piece that was, according to Fontaney, 'infamous in its indecency'. Harel, now manager of the theatre, did his best to bring in the reluctant public. He even inserted a notice in the press:

'It has been noted with surprise that theatres are the only public places where, whatever the number of spectators, no case of cholera has yet been reported. We present this *incontestable* fact for scientific investigation.'

Alexandre Dumas treated the epidemic with healthy disrespect. 'If the plague calls,' he said to Catherine, his maid, 'do not allow it in.' Nevertheless he found himself shivering uncontrollably one day and knew that the cholera had arrived. Hardly knowing what he was doing, he took hold of a wine-glass full of ether, brought to him by the distracted maid, and swallowed it down. He survived this drastic treatment, which he describes in his memoirs under the heading: 'I invent etherisation.'

*　　*　　*

Dumas was still in bed when Harel came to call. 'Ah, my friend,' said the theatre manager, 'what a wonderful time to launch a new play!' With the dying down of the cholera, he explained, there was bound to be a reaction in favour of public entertainments. He had in hand the makings of a huge success, *La Tour de Nesle*, a play by an unknown young author, Frédéric Gaillardet. It only needed re-arranging by a more experienced dramatist. Would Dumas undertake the task? Dumas, protesting that he was half-dead, allowed himself to be persuaded, and Harel left him triumphantly with a final admonition: 'Mind you take trouble with the part for George.'

The tower of the title, a gloomy edifice overlooking the Seine, was the setting, in the play, for nightly orgies held by the queen, Marguerite de Bourgogne, and her sisters. Each night young men, freshly arrived in Paris and so without friends to enquire for them, are lured to the tower by a veiled old serving woman; each morning, murdered to ensure their silence, they are found floating in the river. Horror is piled on horror, incest is added to adultery and murder. *La Tour de Nesle* was melodrama of the blackest kind, more apt to raise a smile than a shudder now, but wholly satisfying to the audiences of the 1830s, still steeped in violent memories of revolution and Napoleon's wars.

Dumas re-wrote the play in three weeks, his imagination carrying him so far, despite his convalescent state, that scarcely a word of the original remained. His co-author, Gaillardet, had accepted the collaboration with some reluctance and Dumas, whether out of consideration for his feelings or because his most recent historical play, *Charles VII et ses Grands Vassaux*, had been savagely treated by the critics and he wished to lie low, announced his intention of remaining anonymous. *La Tour de Nesle* was billed as the work of 'Messieurs Gaillardet et ∗ ∗ ∗'.

The first night, with Mademoiselle George as the adulterous queen, was a wild success. Dumas left Gaillardet to take repeated curtain calls, and returned home well content.* But next morning Harel, who had made an open secret of Dumas' part in the play and wished to take advantage of his celebrity, changed the wording of the play-bill.

'Do you know what Harel has done?' asked one of Dumas' friends who visited him that day.

'What?'

'Instead of proceeding, as in mathematics, from the known to the unknown, he has proceeded from the unknown to the known.'

'I do not understand.'

'Instead of putting "Messieurs Gaillardet et ∗ ∗ ∗" on the play-bill he has put "Messieurs ∗ ∗ ∗ et Gaillardet".'

'Oh, the rascal!' exclaimed Dumas. 'He will get me in trouble with Gaillardet.'

And indeed the indignant Gaillardet, furious at being preceded by the all too celebrated asterisks, brought a lawsuit to have the order on the play-bill changed. Harel was delighted. 'My dear fellow,' he told Dumas, 'we have a great success already; with a touch of scandal we shall have an enormous one.'

The affair of the asterisks became a *cause célèbre*, culminating in a duel between Dumas and his outraged co-author two years later. The scandal, as Harel had foreseen, set the seal on the success of the play, which had more than three hundred performances in the next three years, a run which even Hugo could not equal. Financially, *La Tour de Nesle* was the greatest triumph of romantic drama. But the very quality of its success, relying as it did on sensationalism and a surrounding scandal, marked a departure from the high ideals with which the revolution in the theatre had begun three years before. As drama descended into melodrama the hearts which had beat for *Antony* and *Hernani* began to lose their ardour. In literature, as in politics, the process of disillusion was beginning.

* He had contracted with Harel for 10% of the takings.

*   *   *

With the waning of the cholera a fresh outbreak of disturbances began in France. In the Vendée the Duchesse de Berry, claiming the throne on behalf of her son, the grandson of Charles X, launched a short-lived rebellion in May—a rising which ended in farce when the Duchess, captured and imprisoned by the government, was found to be pregnant. She was obliged to reveal her secret marriage to an Italian count and, considered discredited by this *mésalliance*, was shortly afterwards released.

In June the funeral of the liberal General Lamarque, a victim of the cholera, was the pretext for a republican insurrection in Paris in the course of which more than eight hundred people were killed and the defeated rebels summarily executed. Louis-Philippe, displaying exemplary sang-froid, personally supervised the conduct of his troops. 'He was not audacious,' wrote Dumas, 'but he was brave.'

Dumas, whose sympathies, openly and indiscreetly expressed, had been with the rebels, was denounced as a republican after the insurrection, one journal going so far as to publish an account of his court-martial and execution by a firing squad. The news provoked a charming note from Charles Nodier:

'My dear Alexandre—
   I have just read in a newspaper that you were shot on June 6th at three in the morning. Be so good as to tell me if this will prevent you from coming to dine tomorrow at the Arsenal...
           Your very good friend,
           Charles Nodier,
who will be delighted to have the opportunity of asking you for news of the other world.'

Louis-Philippe preserved an indulgent attitude to Dumas, while refusing to take his political opinions seriously. 'My dear Dumas,' he had said, when Dumas had attempted to advise him in an interview the year before, 'politics are a dreary metier. You are a poet. Concentrate on writing poetry... Leave politics to the king and his minister.' Now, in the politest possible manner, he let it be suggested that Dumas should leave Paris for a few months, in order to escape arrest. Dumas took the hint, spending a pleasant summer travelling in Switzerland, writing delightfully about his experiences there and returning that autumn to find himself so far forgiven that the king and the royal family had attended *La Tour de Nesle*.

*   *   *

Alfred de Vigny, recovering slowly and painfully from cholera, had remained aloof from the fighting in the streets. The revolution of 1830 had destroyed his political illusions. Hating violence, he was prepared to play his role in keeping order, serving his turn in the National Guard.* But his views on government were pragmatic. 'One owes neither love nor hate to those who govern; one owes them only the feelings one would have for a coachman: either he drives well or badly, that is all.'

His novel *Stello*, published that summer, expressed his sense of disillusion. Its theme, an obsessive one in his work, was the loneliness of genius. Whatever the political system the poet will always be an outcast and a pariah. Gilbert, starved to death under the *ancien régime*, Chatterton, driven to suicide under a constitutional monarchy, André Chénier, guillotined during the French Revolution, are all the victims of a society which would not understand them.

The novel is cast in the form of a dialogue between Stello, a beautiful youth steeped in romantic dissatisfaction, and the Docteur Noir, an enigmatic figure who prescribes for Stello's melancholy a series of stories or 'Consultations', told through a stifling summer night while Stello tosses on his couch. The first two 'Consultations', those concerning Gilbert and Chatterton, are relatively slight. The third, the longest and the most dramatic, deals with André Chénier. Through his own family and through the reminiscences of his parents' friends, Vigny had imbibed the experience of the Terror, an experience reinforced by extensive reading. The atmosphere of the period is poignantly and powerfully evoked: the prison of Saint-Lazare, the frivolity and heroism of the victims, the blind accidents of chance which make even Robespierre and Saint-Just not masters but tools of fate. 'I feel,' wrote Vigny of this episode, 'that my narrative must be as strong and swift as the blade that is lifted still smoking from a severed head.'

Stello, wrote the critic Gustave Planche, was the 'most spontaneous, the most personal, the most passionate of novels', and Vigny's discerning contemporaries, notably the editor Buloz, who first published it in the *Revue des Deux Mondes*, were quick to acclaim it. But it was too original, too hard to classify, to be a popular success. 'It has given the critics vertigo,' noted Vigny in his journal. 'The lesser journalists, accustomed to judge a book by its cover and its preface, have been blown completely off course.'

Conscious of being misjudged, he took refuge in an attitude of lofty silence. All around him his more prolific contemporaries were producing new works. Vigny had his own concept of creation: 'In poetry, in

* The citizen-militia created by Louis-Philippe.

philosophy, in all literary creation, when one has only enough time to think and write one is lost. One must also have the time to dream.' Gravely and without haste he waited for the tide of inspiration to rise again. His enemies mocked him for the parsimony of his production. Even Musset, who loved him, sketched him as a 'constipated swan'.

Sainte-Beuve, who for all his honeyed words had no warm feelings for him, struck a new blow at Vigny's self-esteem that autumn when in an article in the *Revue des Deux Mondes* he proclaimed the primacy of Victor Hugo in every field of literature: 'Drama, fiction, poetry, all spring today from this great writer who is no less supreme in prose than in poetry.'

Vigny and Hugo had marched side by side in the romantic battle. Vigny's *Cinq-Mars* had preceded *Notre-Dame de Paris*, his *Othello*, *Hernani*. In poetry too he could claim to have led the way. 'The sole merit of these compositions which has never been disputed,' he wrote in the preface to his collected poems, 'is to have been the first of their kind in France in which a philosophic thought is clothed in a dramatic or epic form.' The suggestion that his work, in any way, derived from that of Victor Hugo was an affront too great to pass over. He demanded a retraction from the editor of the *Revue*. Sainte-Beuve, at the editor's insistence, was forced to modify his statement in a subsequent issue.

He would take his revenge for this humiliation,* at first in secret, in a letter to Victor Hugo. 'I understand', he wrote, 'that you have heard of the miseries of a *gentleman* of our acquaintance. A man who can go to such lengths is fit for nothing but satire; his genius and his inspiration are dead. More prolific talents are spared such sordid stratagems.'

'The *gentleman*,' agreed Hugo, 'indeed passes all belief, but what can you expect? One should pity him rather than blame him. He will be delighted if my *Roi s'amuse* is a flop; it is thus that he'll repay my frantic applause at *Othello*.'

'Vigny has two reasons to dislike me,' wrote Hugo in a private note that year. '*Primo* because *Marion de Lorme* has made more money than *La Maréchale d'Ancre*, and *Hernani* more than *Othello*. *Secundo* because I sometimes give my arm to Marie Dorval.'

*   *   *

Hugo gave his arm to Marie Dorval. Even in the first and happiest stage of their love Vigny suffered agonies of jealousy. 'The men she had loved were constantly before my eyes,' he wrote. 'They filled me with horror.' The theatre itself, with its avid audiences was a threat:

---

* In March 1840, in an article on the romantic school, entitled 'Dix ans après en Littérature', in the *Revue des Deux Mondes*, Sainte-Beuve omitted all mention of Vigny's name.

Oh! l'encens du théâtre est un encens impur.
En haut l'acteur brillant, en bas le peuple obscur,
L'un parmi les flambeaux, l'autre dans la poussière
Entament dans la nuit une lutte grossière . . .

But he watched her, entranced, as she prepared to go on stage: 'An actress who is truly inspired is delightful to observe in her dressing-room before a performance. She talks with delicious exaggeration of anything and everything, she flares up for nothing, cries, groans, laughs, sighs, grows angry or caressing in a moment. She says she is ill, suffering, cured, well, weak, strong, gay, melancholy, angry; and she is none of these, she is like a little race-horse at the starting tape, prancing with impatience . . .'

Seven years with Lydia, somnolent, fat and ailing, though even-tempered and good-natured, had left Vigny starved of passion and excitement. With Marie Dorval he found a glorious sensual abandon, a response as vibrant as Lydia's had been dull. He found too a woman whom the hardships and struggles of a miserable youth had left permanently unstable. If Vigny was ravished by her gaiety, her spontaneity and her ardour, he was disquieted by the violence of her sudden rages and despairs. He was made uneasy too by the bohemian circle with which she was surrounded. The apartment of her complaisant husband, Toussaint Merle, was a meeting place for writers, actors and former lovers; Piccini, the father of her youngest child, was a welcome visitor. Vigny remained stiff and formal in the midst of their noise and gaiety; he had a habit of remarking, 'C'est charmant', noted a fellow guest, which was perfectly ridiculous.

The flat was small. To escape from the crowd in the drawing-room Vigny would retire to Marie Dorval's room next door under the pretence of reading aloud to her.

Il faut tenir un livre
Et de nos yeux le suivre
Ouvert sur nos genoux;
Il faut parler et rire
Ou qu'on m'entende lire;
Et quand ma voix expire
Vous frémissez pour nous.

Votre porte est peu close
Et de son rideau rose
Le voile est si léger
Qu'on entend toute chose,

Un fauteuil qui se pose,
Un soupir, une pause,
Et je suis l'étranger;

Et je suis *la visite*,
Et si ma voix hésite
Dans l'éternel babil,
Si par mon imprudence
Quelqu'un en défiance
Entendait mon silence,
Il dirait: 'Que fait-il?'

Puisqu'on nous environne
Sur un ton monotone
Je vais toujours parler,
J'aurai l'air de poursuivre,
Mais d'eux je me délivre.
Et c'est un autre livre
Que je vais dérouler:

C'est mon coeur, c'est mon âme,
C'est l'amour d'une femme
Dans un homme allumé;
Désir, délire, transe,
Ennui, rage, espérance,
Enfin . . . une démence
Qui vaut d'être enfermé . . .

Sens-tu la terre émue?
Ta chambre qui remue?
Vois-tu pas l'ombre aux cieux?
Le jour fuit la nature,
Où donc est ta ceinture?
Va, poursuis ta lecture,
J'ai la nuit sur mes yeux.

Ah! tes cheveux frémissent
Et malgré toi s'unissent
Aux cheveux de mon front;
Ah! ta joue est brûlante
Sur ma lèvre tremblante;
Ah! de ma fièvre lente
Que l'incendie est prompt!

Ils sont là qui m'écoutent,
Qui soupçonnent, qui doutent,

Ils sont tous, ils sont là.
Mais vaine est la contrainte,
Ton coeur a mon empreinte,
Et malgré notre crainte
Je t'ai dit tout cela.

Such snatched delights were soon not enough and Vigny hired a room in the Rue Montaigne, not far from his own apartment, where they could be alone in peace. 'Love, with its furtive glances and its secret rendezvous, uplifts a man and a woman,' he wrote. 'Even though all is permitted to them in marriage they sleep and wake up coldly.'

But before long a new shadow cast itself across the path of love, a shadow that though masculine in outline, with trousers and a tilted top hat, was not that of a man. It was that of George Sand.

*   *   *

George Sand or, divested of her literary disguise, Aurore Dudevant, the wife of a provincial nobleman, had arrived in Paris the year before, leaving her husband and two children behind, to seek emancipation and a wider life. She had set up house, on a meagre allowance, with her lover Jules Sandeau; together, under the name Jules Sand, they had published a novel *Rose et Blanche*. In 1832, writing as George Sand, she had made her name with her first unaided novel, *Indiana*. Chateaubriand, Balzac and Sainte-Beuve sang its praises. Its eloquent attack on marriage and defence of the sovereign claims of love established her at once as a 'new woman'—an image which her favourite garb of trousers, short jacket and top hat did nothing to dispel.

Early that year, moved by an impulse of 'profound sympathy', she had written an admiring letter to Marie Dorval. Ever impetuous—she had first met Dumas by hailing him from a cab—Marie Dorval had burst into George Sand's garret room the next day, exclaiming breathlessly, 'Well, here I am!' An immediate friendship sprang up between the two women, Marie Dorval, the 'essence of feminine disquiet',* and the cigar-smoking George.

Vigny met her at Marie Dorval's apartment. 'She is a woman of about twenty-five,' he noted in his journal. 'She looks like the famous Judith in the gallery. Her black curling hair falls over her shoulders in the manner of one of Raphael's angels. Her eyes are large and black, shaped like those you find in mystics or in the most magnificent Italian heads. Her face is severe and impassive, the mouth badly formed. Her bearing

* George Sand's description.

is ungraceful, her manner abrupt. She resembles a man in her voice and manner and in the forthrightness of her opinions.'

'I can't yet place this woman,' he wrote a little later. 'She goes to see her husband in the country from time to time and lives in Paris with her lover . . . Her daughter is called Solange.'

But he scented danger. 'My Sappho,' he called his mistress in his journal. Arsène Houssaye, in his memoirs, displayed no doubts as to the relationship between the two women, allowing his imagination full rein as he described their amorous exchanges, exchanges of which, by their very nature, he could not have been a witness. Innocent or not, however, gossip made much of the friendship, enhancing Marie Dorval's already scandalous reputation. 'I entrust you to the protection of *your love, your honour and your goodness*,' wrote Vigny to his mistress after a scene of furious jealousy. Seldom has trust been more misplaced. 'On what a breast,' sneered Sainte-Beuve, 'has this tear of Christ alighted!'

*   *   *

Sainte-Beuve had his own emotional preoccupations that year, subdued and subfusc compared to Vigny's. 'My beloved Adèle,' runs a letter, 'how good and beautiful you were yesterday, and how that half-hour in the corner of the chapel leaves eternal and delicious memories! My friend, it is fourteen years since I had been there; and I went there, fourteen years ago, also with profound and tender emotion. I was very pious in those days. It was the first year of my arrival in Paris and my heart was sick with longing for my mother and home. I was working very hard at college, and all the time that I was not working, every moment of freedom or recreation, I spent in weeping. It was in this little chapel above all that the tears came most readily. There was a psalm in the prayer-book that I used to read and re-read, *Super flumen Babylonis*, when the Hebrew captives sat down by the water, weeping as they remembered Zion and refusing to play their harps in an alien land . . .

'At that time, which I recalled yesterday, two people in the world loved me inexpressibly, an old aunt above all, and my mother. My old aunt is dead, and you have replaced her, loving me as much as she did but more spontaneously; your young kisses have replaced hers; soon, when my mother is no more, they will be all that remain to me . . .'

Did Adèle Hugo yield to Sainte-Beuve? Her letters to him—more than 350 of them—were destroyed after his death, and of his to her only occasional copies found in his papers remain. References in letters to his friends and even in the *Livre d'Amour* leave the matter ambiguous. But Sainte-Beuve's love for Adèle, whether it stopped short of total possession or not, was the one great passion of his life and, for a time at least, reciprocated.

The Hugos spent that summer in the country, staying with their friends the Bertins* at the Château des Roches near the valley of Bièvre. Hugo, who had been suffering from headaches and an inflammation of the eyes brought on by overwork, found solace in the peace of the country and in the company of his children, Léopoldine, the eldest, a gentle, studious child of eight, being his especial joy. He constructed little boats and carriages out of paper for them, painting and gilding them with meticulous delicacy. Adèle Hugo, at last recovered from the ill health and crises of the previous year, was, he wrote in a friendly letter to Sainte-Beuve, putting on weight visibly and walking five miles a day. The walks were not so innocent as he supposed: the little romanesque church of Bièvre provided another of those crepuscular meeting places so dear to Sainte-Beuve.

In October, shortly after their return to Paris, the Hugos moved house once more, this time to a splendid apartment in the seventeenth-century Place-Royale (now the Place des Vosges). Hugo describes himself as hard at work hammering and nailing, furnishing the apartment with dark red damask, Venetian mirrors and sombre gothic and Renaissance furniture.

At the same time he was in the throes of supervising the rehearsals for his new play *Le Roi s'amuse*, later the basis of Verdi's opera *Rigoletto*. Sainte-Beuve, who had listened to its reading at the Théâtre Français, wrote to Victor Pavie: 'The story is of François I and Triboulet. Triboulet has a charming and mysterious daughter whom the king debauches without knowing who she is. The result is the grief and despair of the poor jester . . . I have a number of little opinions of my own on this type of drama and its degree of naturalness and human truth but I have no doubt of the impression that will be produced and of the immense talent displayed in this work, which is radiant with beautiful poetry.'

Though Hugo's home was still banned to Sainte-Beuve when Adèle was present the friends had remained in amicable correspondence that year. In the eyes of the world Sainte-Beuve was still Hugo's greatest friend and enjoyed the reflected glow of his fame. Sainte-Beuve's own reputation was growing and Hugo, all personal affections apart, knew the value of his influence as a critic. Sainte-Beuve now hastened to offer his services for *Le Roi s'amuse*. Hugo's claque was ready, with Théophile Gautier at its head, but it was smaller than on previous occasions and he was uneasy about the composition of the rest of the audience. 'All

* Louis-François Bertin was editor of the *Journal des Débats*.

the seats in the theatre have been taken, my friend,' he wrote to Sainte-Beuve, 'but how and by whom I am not too sure.'

On the evening of the first performance, only minutes before the curtain rose, came the news of an assassination attempt on Louis-Philippe. The king had been fired at as he crossed the Pont Royal; he had reacted with his usual bravery, bending low over his horse's neck to avoid the shot and straightening up immediately afterwards to wave to the crowd. The audience, excited and distracted by rumours, were not in a receptive mood, and the efforts of Hugo's claque failed to whip up enthusiasm for the drama taking place on the stage. Whether from ill-will or inefficiency the actors showed themselves particularly inept that evening: lines were forgotten; the abduction of the jester's daughter was greeted with catcalls; a series of ridiculous incidents—a door that failed to open, a blindfold that slipped off—ruined Hugo's best effects. The evening ended amidst jeers and hisses. Hugo returned home through the pouring rain in deepest gloom.

Next morning the government suspended his play, on the pretext of its immorality. Their real reason was that the action, in which the jester plots to kill the king, was an incitement to regicide. Hugo protested eloquently, turning the setback, with his usual skill, into an occasion for publicity. '*Le Roi s'amuse* has been suspended by the government,' wrote Fontaney. 'What a service to Victor! He plays his role superbly. They've taken 20,000 francs from his pocket!'

Two years after the revolution the censor was back in control. The attempted shooting of Louis-Philippe had done much to consolidate the king's position, and his personal popularity was considerably increased by his bravery under fire. The crushing of the republican insurrection in June and the discrediting of the Duchesse de Berry and the legitimist cause had removed two important threats to his régime that year. In July too the Duc de Reichstadt, Napoleon's son, had died at Schönbrunn and with him the immediate hopes of the Bonapartist party. To a public tired of violence and uncertainty Louis-Philippe, though he satisfied few of the profounder aspirations of the revolution, seemed to provide the best hope of stability. Delacroix's famous painting 'Liberty Guiding the People' had symbolised the spirit of 1830. Its fate was equally symbolic. Exhibited at the Salon of 1831, it had been bought by the state as a sop to popular opinion and almost immediately relegated to an attic. It would not reappear until 1848.

'A republic will come,' wrote Victor Hugo in his notebook for that year, 'and when it comes it will be good. But let us not pick fruit in May which will not be ripe until July; let us know how to wait.'

7

1833

Hugo did not repine for long at the failure of *Le Roi s'amuse*. He had written another play in the summer of 1832, his first in prose, *Le Souper à Ferrare*. A melodrama as sensational in its effects as *La Tour de Nesle*, its climax was a banquet offered by Lucrezia Borgia to her enemies, interrupted at its height by a chanting procession of monks who have come to offer the last rites to the guests. At the end of the year Harel had come to call on Hugo.

'I've just read *Le Roi s'amuse*,' he told him. 'It is magnificent. Only the Théâtre Français could have managed to make it flop. I've come to ask you for *Le Souper à Ferrare*.'

Hugo, displeased with the Théâtre Français, which he felt had accepted the censor's ban too easily, was content to take his revenge at the Porte-Saint-Martin. Mademoiselle George was the natural choice for the part of Lucrezia Borgia and Harel, ever anxious to please his famous mistress, begged the author to change the title of the play to that of its leading character. Hugo agreed: the title became *Lucrèce Borgia*.

But it was not Mademoiselle George, robed though she was in the glory of her Napoleonic past and far from indifferent to Hugo's attractions, who took Hugo's eye at the rehearsals. Juliette Drouet, a young actress somewhat equivocally under Harel's wing, had begged for the part of Princess Negroni. It was only a minor role, but Juliette Drouet was not perturbed. 'There are no small parts in a play by Victor Hugo,' she announced. Her languishing glances at the author did not pass unnoticed by the rest of the cast. Hugo remained scrupulously formal and polite, addressing her always as 'Mademoiselle Juliette' and kissing her hand ceremoniously when he made his departure from the theatre. 'It's enough to make you die of laughter,' exclaimed Frédérick Lemaître, who was playing opposite Mademoiselle George.

Juliette Drouet was twenty-six. She had had many lovers, by one of whom, the sculptor Charles Pradier, she had had a daughter. Her chief protector, at the opening of 1833, was the Russian prince Anatole Demidoff, who supported her in a luxury appropriate to her astonishing beauty. Although she was an indifferent actress, her looks had already made her celebrated—a figure whose classical proportions had inspired the sculptures of her lover Pradier, an oval face whose delicate features and gentle eyes showed no trace of the hardness that might be expected in one whose career had been that of a courtesan. And in fact, launched into the *demi-monde* almost by accident, after a convent upbringing, Juliette had never acquired the cynicism appropriate to her role. 'It seems to me,' she had written to a lover, 'that my soul has its desires as well as my body, and a thousand times more ardent . . . I would leave you, I would abandon you, the world and life itself, if I could find a man whose soul would caress my soul, as you caress and love my body.'

The first night of *Lucrèce Borgia*, on February 2nd, was a triumph to expunge the failure of *Le Roi s'amuse*. The generous Dumas, tears of delight in his eyes, rushed to clasp the hand of Madame Hugo in the entr'acte. Frédérick Lemaître and Mademoiselle George were superb in their *élan*. But Hugo preserved the vision above all of Juliette Drouet, swanlike in pink and silver damask with a nodding head-dress of pearls and plumes.

Every evening, after the performance, drawn by the promise in her dark eyes, he would go round to congratulate her in her dressing-room. On February 19th, for the first time, they spent the night together. It was the beginning of a love that would last for fifty years, its anniversary religiously remembered.

'Beloved one, do you remember?' wrote Hugo in 1841. 'Our first night! It was a carnival night—Shrove Tuesday, 1833. There was a ball at one of the theatres and we were both to have gone to it. (I interrupt myself to kiss you, and now I go on.) The hours of that night pass through my memory even now, like stars before the eyes of my soul. You were to have gone to the ball, and you did not go. You waited for me instead, an angel of beauty and love.

'What a delicious silence reigned in your little room. Outside we heard Paris laugh and sing, and the masqueraders passing to and fro. In the midst of the general festivities we held our own celebration, set apart and hidden in the shadows. Paris enjoyed a false intoxication, we the true one.'

News of Hugo's new attachment quickly spread around Paris. Hugo, the model husband, who lived, said Flaubert, 'like a bourgeois while thinking like a demigod', now came home at all hours and sometimes not at all. The humiliations he had suffered at the hands of Adèle, who resolutely kept herself in a separate bedroom, were forgotten in Juliette's passionate embraces and her equally passionate admiration for his poetry. Hugo did not conceal his delight at his new conquest, justifying himself however to anxious friends.

'Never have I been guilty of so many faults as I have been this year,' he wrote to Victor Pavie, 'and yet never have I been a better man. I am a far better man now than in that time of *innocence* that you regret.

Formerly I was innocent; now I am indulgent. There is great progress there, God knows.

'I have beside me a good and dear friend, an angel who knows it too, whom you venerate and who loves me and forgives me. To love and to forgive—that is more than mere man can accomplish. It is a task for God—and for woman.'

Adèle Hugo had more reasons to be indulgent than Hugo realised. Sainte-Beuve rejoiced at the liaison for her sake:

> . . . car ta prison est enfin adoucie,
> Car lui, le dur jaloux, l'orgueilleux offensé,
> S'est pris au piège aussi d'un amour insensé,
> Il court nuit et jour après l'objet qui l'enlève;
> Et nous, prompts à jouir de chaque courte trève,
> Nous courons non moins vite aux bois les plus voisins . . .

*   *   *

Sainte-Beuve's devotion to Adèle was a continuing passion, but 1833 saw the beginning of a new relationship, albeit a cautious one, with a woman. He had need to be cautious. The woman was George Sand.

Literary Paris was small. Sainte-Beuve had reviewed *Indiana* and *Valentine*, the novel that followed it, in admiring terms. It was not surprising that George Sand should wish to thank him and that she should ask a mutual friend to bring him to call. An immediate if not a total sympathy sprang up between the two. 'At that delicate moment in her life when she was just becoming famous,' wrote Sainte-Beuve, 'she turned to me as a confidant, a counsellor, almost a confessor.'

George Sand was restless and unhappy. She had just shaken off her lover, Jules Sandeau, the first half of whose surname had given her her pseudonym. With an optimism that would persist through many disappointments she was searching once more for a lover who would correspond to her ideals, and satisfy both her senses and her soul. Her novel *Lélia*, published that summer, describes that fruitless quest. Lélia, thirsting for the infinite, passes vainly from lover to lover, frustrated always by an 'ardour of the spirit which paralyses the senses before they are ever awoken': in other words she is frigid. Sainte-Beuve was impressed and slightly nervous: 'To be a woman, to be less than thirty, to have plumbed such abysses and yet to show no outward sign; to possess such knowledge—knowledge that would seam our brow and turn our hair to grey—to carry it with such lightness, ease and sobriety in the writing: *that* is what I admire.'

George Sand invited him to supper and he stayed till dawn the next morning while she read her novel to him. But their orgy, he told a friend, confined itself to drinking coffee. He had no desire to test the depths that Lélia had plumbed. Instead he offered to introduce her to Alfred de Musset, or some other suitable young man. She refused: Musset, she said, was too much of a dandy for her liking. In any case she was beginning to be interested in a new acquaintance, Prosper Mérimée. Mérimée was a cynic in matters of love; he prided himself on his technical expertise. 'The strength of his personality fascinated me,' she wrote to Sainte-Beuve. 'For eight days I believed that he knew the secret of happiness, that he would teach it to me, that his scornful insouciance would cure my childish susceptibilities.'

The experiment with Mérimée was a disaster. Their first and only night together was a fiasco, her lack of modesty, according to Mérimée, killing all desire in him. He covered his chagrin by mocking at her. She wept from nervous exhaustion, disgust and discouragement. 'At the age of thirty,' she wrote to Sainte-Beuve, 'I behaved as no fifteen-year-old girl would have done.'

She confided her story to Marie Dorval whose freedom from inhibition she had longed to emulate. Marie Dorval, not always discreet, passed it on to Dumas, who repeated it all round Paris, and to the disapproving Vigny. 'This monstrous woman,' he wrote in his journal, 'told her new friend yesterday: "Well, it's over; I gave myself yesterday to ——". She had this man who despised her and who said so. She added: "He treated me like a tart. He said: 'You behave like a tart without having the advantages of being one, you are as proud as a marquise with none of a marquise's graces.' " '

*   *   *

Vigny's suspicion of George Sand had deepened into dislike. The theme of Lesbos was one that had haunted him as a young man; it would recur again in his anathemas against women in 'La Colère de Samson':

> Bientôt, se retirant dans un hideux royaume,
> La Femme aura Gomorrhe et l'Homme aura Sodome,
> Et, se jetant de loin un regard irrité,
> Les deux sexes mourront chacun de son côté.

'Madame Sand comes to see one of her friends at midnight and wants to spend the night with her. Bizarre conversation,' he noted in his journal. And later, at the foot of a letter which Marie Dorval had received from George Sand, while she was on tour in the provinces, begging to join her there: 'I have forbidden Marie to answer this Lesbian who pesters her.'

Pursued by the debts incurred by her husband and daughters, Marie Dorval spent much of that year on tour in a desperate effort to make money quickly. Vigny was unable to follow her. At the beginning of March his mother had suffered an apoplectic stroke. Already committed to nursing his wife, he now faced the burden of caring for his mother whose reason for the time being had gone and whose violent bouts of anger made the task of those looking after her doubly difficult. Marie Dorval's letters to him, describing her triumphs in the provinces, provoked a bitter response. 'You live in the midst of gaieties and pleasures,' wrote Vigny, 'and I in a sort of hospital.' The accusation was unfair: the life of a strolling player, even one so fêted as Marie, was hard and gruelling. Her debts were a continual worry, fatigue and illness dogged her, she was uneasy about her daughters, above all, she wrote to Vigny, she suffered from terrible jealousy on his behalf, a jealousy that included his 'odious wife', and a fear that he might grow weary of her in her absence.

In May she made a brief return to Paris to play at a benefit performance at the Opéra in Vigny's *Quitte pour la Peur*, a 'pastel sketch', he wrote, 'in the manner of Boucher or Watteau', in which she played the role of an eighteenth-century duchess. Vigny had written the part expressly for her. He hated to see her frittering away her talents in the second-rate melodramas of the Porte-Saint-Martin and had been trying for some time to obtain her a place at the Théâtre Français, but the hatred and antagonism of the other players had so far blocked the way to a satisfactory engagement. Despite his efforts Marie Dorval reproached him for not doing enough to further her career.

'Ah! what cruelty to accuse me, me! of not having done enough to serve you in the theatre,' wrote Vigny. 'You know what my life has been, how could I have done more? You will see, if you will only let me trust you, what I shall do for you . . .'

*   *   *

'How all that was fair, flourishing and capable of growth a few years ago has withered,' wrote Sainte-Beuve that year. '. . . All our poets in decline, all our idols fallen. Hugo, the author of 'Son nom' and 'A toi', at the feet of Juliette; Eloa the captive and victim of Madame Dorval . . . Oh! it is only we, my Adèle, who have followed our destiny—let us cling to one another until death and beyond it! I love you.'

He was working on a novel, *Volupté*, whose theme, veiled and almost dreamlike, was the story of his relationship with the Hugos. His was a nature, he told George Sand, little inclined to hope. 'I have lost the energy for happiness like ground too long soaked with water which remains damp and cold even when the sun appears.' His feeling for Adèle Hugo, his book itself, were impregnated with the same sense of lassitude and melancholy, and in his description of the hero, Amaury's, break with M. de Couaen, the character who stands for Hugo, he wrote the epilogue to the friendship which had meant so much to him. 'Absent, this vital man would always carry with him a large part of myself. I left in his heart a bleeding tatter of my own, as Milon left his limbs in an oak, and I bore the fragments of his heart in my own flesh.'

The painful break foreshadowed in his novel had not yet taken place but already there were signs of disintegration. Sainte-Beuve had seen little of Hugo in the first months of the year. Hugo was caught up with his new love for Juliette Drouet and his salon, where he still received with his wife, remained forbidden to Sainte-Beuve. The continuing embargo was a lively source of bitterness. Sainte-Beuve's resentment burst out that summer when in an article by one of Hugo's circle he was accused of fickleness in his affections, both personal and literary.

'For a long time now,' he wrote to Hugo, 'those who come to your home, amazed in the end at never seeing me there, have been hard put to find an explanation. The simplest, the most convenient and the most specious is undoubtedly this: "he is fickle, inconstant in his affections". The most important fact in my life having been my declared and devoted affection for you, the most striking impression given at present must be that of my fickleness and inconstancy.' Hugo well knew, he went on, the reason for this so-called inconstancy, yet he did nothing to dispel the impression given, even allowing it to be repeated in print. He was forced to conclude that their friendship, on the terms it had formerly existed, had come to an end. It only remained to preserve the decencies at its demise.

Hugo wrote back with sorrow and affection. The misunderstandings between them, enlarged by distance and hearsay, would evaporate in less than half an hour of talk. 'You know my nature little, Sainte-Beuve, you have always believed that I live by the intellect but I live only by the heart. To love and to need *love* and *friendship*, use which word you prefer, is the mainspring of my life, happy or unhappy, public or private, wounded or whole. You have never sufficiently recognised this in me . . . I admit that absence has produced inverse effects in us two. You love me less than two years ago, I love you more. On reflection the reason is simple. It was I who was afflicted. The slow and gradual process of forgetting on both sides, the reasons which separated us works in your favour in my heart and against me in yours. Since life is like this let us resign ourselves to it . . .

'The attachment on my side was still so strong that your letter, announcing that I no longer had a friend, leaves me shattered and cut to the quick. The wound will be long in healing. Goodbye. I am always yours from the bottom of my heart. My one consolation in this life is that I have never been the first to leave a heart that loved me.'

Once more, and for the last time, Sainte-Beuve drew back from the brink. He wrote to make his peace: 'Thank you, my friend, for your letter,' replied Hugo. 'Thank you even for the first letter since it has brought me the second . . . Do not imagine that I have not suffered much on your behalf in the last two years. You have often misjudged me because of my calm exterior . . . Oh! Sainte-Beuve, two friends like us should never grow apart.'

Hugo's life was more hectic than ever that summer. He was completing another play, *Marie Tudor*, for the Porte-Saint-Martin. Juliette Drouet had not yet been tamed to her role of devoted slave. She was still being supported in luxury by Prince Demidoff; to separate herself from him was a sacrifice that in the early months, deeply in love though she was, she was not prepared to make. Hugo was furiously jealous, there were scenes, quarrels and reconciliations. Twice Juliette attempted to break off their relations and to leave Paris; each time he pursued her and brought her back.

His *Marie Tudor*, he hoped, would give her the opportunity she longed for in the theatre and with it financial independence. The play, like *Lucrèce Borgia*, would have Mademoiselle George in the leading role; for Juliette he had written a part of almost equal importance, Jane Talbot, a 'gazelle' to Marie Tudor's 'panther'.

The rehearsals were bedevilled from the first by backstage intrigues. Dumas and Hugo had always had rival parties in the theatre and among the public, but until now, each too self-confident to fear competition, had remained firm friends. Once more the trouble was caused by an article—an attack on Dumas by a friend of Hugo's in the *Journal des Débats*, accusing him of plagiarism. Hugo was commonly held, though he denied it, to have inspired the article. Dumas took offence. 'The two friends,' wrote Sainte-Beuve, 'have fallen out for ever, and, what is worse, causing scandal: which brings the state of poetry into disrepute.'

The quarrel re-echoed in the theatre, dividing the actors and increasing the antagonism which Juliette, as Hugo's *protégée*, had to meet at rehearsals. Mademoiselle George had no liking for younger, prettier actresses, and the leading actor, Bocage, a friend of Dumas, treated Juliette with such insolence that Hugo withdrew his role from him. Poor Juliette's confidence drained away; she was paralysed, she wrote, by the enmity she encountered.

The first night, November 6th, was a humiliating nightmare for

Juliette Drouet. She was completely eclipsed by Mademoiselle George. Her voice was almost inaudible, her movements lacked assurance, she stood for much of the play with her head bowed so low that she looked, said a critic, as if she were searching for a pin that had fallen from her dress. The audience, many of them hostile to Hugo, who did not have his usual claque, hissed her unmercifully.

Hugo's friends, Sainte-Beuve among them, begged him to save the play by replacing Juliette Drouet by a more experienced actress. There was one already waiting. Dumas, like Hugo, had his *protégée* at the Porte-Saint-Martin. Anticipating Juliette's failure, she had already learnt the part. Juliette, crushed and genuinely ill, pleaded an indisposition and withdrew from the play. Hugo consoled her tenderly, praising her performance, but could not fail to realise that Dumas' mistress, Ida Ferrier, though far less good-looking, was more of a match for Mademoiselle George, tigerish and magnificent as the English queen.

*   *   *

Ida Ferrier was a match for Dumas too. She had ousted the black-haired Belle Krelshamer and now reigned efficiently over Dumas' household, entertaining for him with great style and splendour—a fact which, as much as her sensual charms, explained her hold over him, for Dumas loved to keep an open house and lavish table for his innumerable friends. Short, plump, with corn-coloured hair and a perfect complexion, she concealed with an accomplished social manner a jealous and domineering nature to which, once safely established as Dumas' mistress, she gave full expression. She harassed him to further her career on the stage, she poisoned his daily life, interrupting his work, for him the supreme necessity, with jealous scenes. Dumas' friends, who had watched the continuance of his liaison with astonishment, were still more amazed when in 1840 he finally married her. 'My dear fellow,' he told the actor René Luguet who had asked him what could have possessed him, 'it was the only way to get rid of her.'

For Alexandre Dumas *fils* the advent of Ida Ferrier was a crowning misfortune. Belle Krelshamer had at least taken an interest in his welfare; Ida Ferrier, jealous of Dumas' love for his son, did all she could to keep them apart. His life at school had become a misery. In the previous year he had been moved to a new establishment, run by a theatrical friend of his father's, who had collaborated with him on a successful melodrama, *Richard Darlington*—Dumas, at this stage of his career, was producing three or four plays a year. But his father's renown did little for his son. The slur of illegitimacy, and the fact that his mother worked for a living, far outweighed his father's glory as a playwright with his fellow pupils. They tormented him with references to his birth. 'Monsieur,' one would ask the master in class, 'what was the surname of *le beau* Dunois?'

'The bastard of Orléans.'

'And what is a bastard?'

The master would hesitate before the explanation, which the pupils were quick to supply. Obscene drawings of his mother were scribbled on Alexandre's exercise books, and he himself was treated as an object of derision and lewd speculation. 'Do you wish to know the only crime,' he wrote in his novel *Affaire Clémenceau*, in which he gave fictional form to his experiences, 'for which I will never forgive myself or those who drove me to it? It is to have doubted my mother, to have sometimes blushed for her.'

Dumas *père*, taken up with work and his new mistress, saw too little of his son to guess his sufferings. Dumas *fils* adored his father. When he grew up he treated him with almost paternal indulgence: 'My father', he would say, 'is a great big child I had when I was very young.' Nonetheless, he would write with all the intensity of bitter experience: 'I hold that a man who deliberately brings a child into this world (and he cannot do this otherwise than deliberately) without assuring its moral and social well-being, and without recognising his responsibility for the subsequent trouble which his action may cause, is a criminal to be classed somewhere between thieves and murderers.'

*   *   *

Since the fiasco with Mérimée, Sainte-Beuve, obeying the instances of Adèle, had kept at a discreet distance from George Sand. 'Friendship between the sexes,' he told her, 'is only really possible when the adventurous and changing stage of life is over, and both parties, having reached a certain age and with their active life behind them, can sit warming themselves on a bench in the four o'clock sun.' He must have felt a certain relief when in August 1833 he received a letter from her. 'I have fallen in love,' she wrote 'and this time very seriously, with Alfred de Musset . . . I am very happy, thank God on my behalf.'

She had met him at a dinner given by the *Revue des Deux Mondes* for their principal contributors. Alfred de Musset was a recent recruit to the *Revue*. Early that year he had published *Un Spectacle dans un Fauteuil*, a volume that contained the first of his plays for armchair reading, *La Coupe et les Lèvres* and *A quoi rêvent les Jeunes Filles*, and a long poem 'Namouna'. The book had been badly received by the critics; only Sainte-Beuve had praised it in an article for the *Revue des Deux Mondes* and it was through Sainte-Beuve that Musset was shortly afterwards engaged as a contributor.

The dinner had taken place at a restaurant. Musset was placed next to George Sand, the only woman present. She wore a little dagger at her belt; he was struck by her beauty, her olive skin with its bronze highlights, her enormous dark eyes like an Indian's. She found him not at all the dandy she had feared, but charming-looking with his slender figure in a fashionably tight frock coat, his carefully disarranged fair hair, his fine, almost girlish features. George Sand was habitually rather silent in company. Musset, often bored and sullen when only men were present, could be as witty and enchanting as one of his own heroes when women were present. A famous *femme de lettres*, independent and emancipated, was something new in his experience and he put himself out to please her. The evening ended with an invitation on her part, simple and without flirtatiousness, to come and call on her.

Musset re-read her *Indiana*. (Later, he would go through it, crossing out adjectives.) He sent her a poem inspired by reading it, switching from the formal 'vous' of the note that accompanied it to a poetic 'tu'. The subject matter, like that of *Indiana*, was daring:

> Sand, quand tu l'écrivais, où donc l'avais-tu vue,
> Cette scène terrible où Noun, à demi nue
> Sur le lit d'Indiana s'enivre avec Raimond? . . .

Poetic familiarity soon led to real familiarity. Musset came, as George Sand had asked, to call on her in her little flat in the Rue Malaquais. She received him with an air of easy comradeship; she was wearing a négligé and Turkish slippers and smoking a long rosewood pipe. Before long he was a regular visitor, one of the group of young men who surrounded her and whose bohemian gaiety provided a foil to her own somewhat solemn disposition. Musset, habitually dissipated and accustomed to easy conquests, was not used to such platonic friendships.

'You know me well enough,' he wrote to her, 'to be sure that the idiotic question—will you or won't you?—will never cross my lips with you. There is the whole Baltic sea between us in this respect. You have nothing to offer but a chaste love and that is something I can never give (always supposing that if I could you wouldn't send me about my business). But I can, if you think me worthy, be, not even your friend— for that sounds too chaste for me—but a casual comrade, without claims on you, and thus avoiding jealousy or scenes, who can smoke your tobacco, rumple your négligés, and catch a cold in the head philosophising with you under all the chestnut-trees of contemporary Europe . . .'

A few days later he abandoned this pretence: 'My dear George, I have something stupid and ridiculous to tell you . . . You're going to laugh in my face and think that everything I've said till now has been mere phrases. You'll show me the door and you'll think I'm lying. I'm

Victor Hugo in 1829. From a lithograph by Achille Devéria.

Charles Nodier's salon at the Arsenal, 1831.
From an engraving by Tony Johannot.

Charles Augustin Sainte-Beuve in 1831
From an engraving by Demary.

Adèle Hugo c. 1832. From a painting by Louis Boulanger.

Above: Léopoldine Hugo drawn by her mother, April 1837.
Below: 11 Rue Notre-Dame des Champs, Victor Hugo's home
from 1827 to 1830.

Alfred de Vigny in 1831. From a lithograph by Achille Devéria.

Alexandre Dumas in 1829. From a lithograph by Achille Devéria.

'Ballade à la Lune': self-portrait by Alfred de Musset, 1834.

'Ode à la Colonne': frontispiece by Cousin for the
1828 edition of Victor Hugo's *Odes et Ballades*.

'Les Romantiques': a contemporary view of the romantics of the 1830's.

9

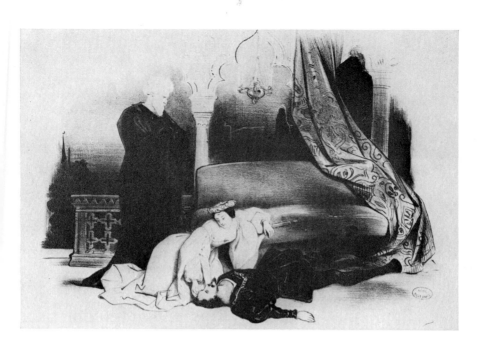

Above: Hernani: the final scene. From a lithograph by Eugène
Devéria. *Below*: Erection of a barricade, July 29, 1830. From
a lithograph by Bellangé.

Juliette Drouet in 1832. From a lithograph by Léon Noël.

Right: Mademoiselle George. From a painting by Gérard. *Below left:* Charles Nodier. From a lithograph by Emile Laselle. *Below right:* Mademoiselle Mars. From a lithograph by Achille Devéria.

Alfred de Musset in 1831. Bronze medallion by David d'Angers.

George Sand drawn by Alfred de Musset, 1833.

Marie Dorval in the role of Marion de Lorme, 1831.
From a lithograph by Achille Devéria.

in love with you. I have been since the first day I came to see you . . .'
And in another letter: 'Have pity on me, do not despise me . . . Let
those who can love, I know only how to suffer . . . Adieu, George, I
love you like a child.'

It was this appeal to her maternal instinct, wrote George Sand, in her
novel *Elle et Lui*, a thinly fictionalised account of her relationship with
Musset, that tipped the balance.

' "Like a child," she repeated, clutching the letter with hands that
trembled with I know not what emotion. "He loves me like a child!
Oh my God, does he know what he is saying—does he know the pain
he is causing me?" '

George Sand was twenty-nine, six years older than Musset. Her two
small children, Maurice, aged eight and at boarding school, and four-
year-old Solange, who was now living with her in Paris, were not, it
seemed, enough to assuage her maternal feelings. A mock incestuous
theme ran through her relationship with Musset, and his with her. She
spoke of him as her 'child', and he at times called her his 'mother' or his
'sister'. But this was only one strand in the complex history of their
love, which in its early days was filled with delight, and in which George
Sand, to her pleasure, found herself 'not altogether Lélia'.

Musset moved into the flat in the Rue Malaquais. The little band of
George's familiars, among them the critic Gustave Planche and the
children's tutor Jules Boucoiran, were at first indignant, then resigned.
Musset drew caricatures of them or tossed off verses in their honour.

> George est dans sa chambrette,
> Entre deux pots de fleurs,
> Fumant sa cigarette,
> Les yeux baignés de pleurs.
>
> Buloz* assis par terre
> Lui fait des doux serments
> Solange, par derrière,
> Gribouille ses romans.
>
> Planté comme une borne,
> Boucoiron tout mouillé
> Contemple d'un oeil morne
> Musset tout débraillé. . .
>
> Planche, saoul de la veille,
> Est assis dans un coin,
> Et se cure l'oreille
> Avec le plus grand soin.

* Editor of the *Revue des Deux Mondes*.

Gaiety reigned in the little flat that summer. George Sand seemed ten years younger, Musset gave vent to his high spirits in pranks and practical jokes. He dressed up as a servant girl at a dinner she gave for colleagues from the *Revue des Deux Mondes*, among them the eminent philosopher Lerminier. The famous pierrot Deburau (immortalised by Jean Louis Barrault in *Les Enfants du Paradis*), had also been invited. He arrived disguised as a visiting British politician, wearing a stiff collar and a long black coat, unrecognisable without his pierrot's costume and his chalk-white make-up. Throughout the dinner he maintained a truly English stiffness, contributing only monosyllables to the conversation. Finally the phrase 'European equilibrium' was mentioned. The laconic Englishman showed a sudden interest.

'Do you wish to know how I view the European equilibrium in the present grave political situation between the continent and England?' he asked. 'If so, I will try to make myself clear.' And, picking up his plate, he spun it up into the air, catching it neatly on the tip of his knife where it continued to rotate at top speed. 'Such', he continued, 'is the present state of the European equilibrium. There can be no salvation without it.'

The astonished guests burst out laughing, the deception was revealed and Alfred de Musset, unable to maintain his servant's role a moment longer, emptied a carafe of water over Lerminier's head.

1833, the year of his meeting with George Sand, was a period of intense creation in Musset's life. His *Spectacle dans un Fauteuil* was followed by two more plays, to be read rather than performed, *Andrea del Sarto* and *Les Caprices de Marianne*. In August his 'Rolla' appeared, a poem memorable for its analysis of the religious drama of his generation. Hugo, emancipated from his earlier orthodoxy, wrote of the 'rotting corpse'* of conventional religion they all carried within them. Musset's hero Rolla, drowning his idealism in debauchery and finally in suicide, sees a world left empty by the loss of faith:

> Je ne crois pas, ô Christ! à ta parole sainte:
> Je suis venu trop tard dans un monde trop vieux . . .
> Ta gloire est morte, ô Christ! et sur nos croix d'ébène
> Ton cadavre céleste est poussière est tombé!
> Eh bien! qu'il soit permis d'en baiser la poussière
> Au moins crédule enfant de ce siècle sans foi,
> Et de pleurer, ô Christ! sur cette froide terre
> Qui vivait de ta mort, et qui mourra sans toi!
> Oh! maintenant, mon Dieu, qui lui rendra la vie?

* Nous portons dans nos coeurs le cadavre pourri
  De la religion qui vivait dans nos pères . . .

Du plus pur de ton sang tu l'avais rajeunie;
Jésus, ce que tu fis, qui jamais le fera?
Nous, vieillards nés d'hier, qui nous rajeunira?

The spirit of Shakespeare, so unsuccessfully evoked elsewhere, breathed through Musset's plays, that of Byron through his poetry. Critics varied in their judgements, but his success among his younger contemporaries seemed confirmed on the evening after 'Rolla's' publication when Musset, leaving the Opéra, tossed his cigar-butt on the ground and saw it picked up by a young man who wrapped it reverently in a piece of paper. No mark of appreciation, wrote Musset's brother, ever gave him greater pleasure.

Towards the end of the summer, when the heat in Paris had become intolerable, George Sand and Musset went to spend a few days at Fontainebleau, leaving her children in the care of her maid with instructions to Gustave Planche to take them to the theatre. They wandered among the woods and rocks near Fontainebleau, George Sand, in a blouse and man's attire, singing at the top of her voice as she strode along the sandy paths. On a moonlit evening, in a clearing surrounded by great limestone rocks, Musset, who had left her to climb in a little ravine, was seized by a terrifying hallucination or brainstorm in which he saw the spectre of himself as a debauched old man, gaunt, wild-haired, with tattered garments, while the echoes of the valley chanted an obscene refrain. He flung himself to the ground to hide his eyes; his despairing screams brought George Sand hurrying to his side. It was not the first hallucination from which he had suffered: five years before, he had described a horrifying encounter with a corpse which had lain across him in his bed, covering his face with kisses smelling of corruption. The fit had passed, as it did now, very quickly, and the next morning Musset was ready to joke about it, even to draw caricatures of his affrighted mistress. George Sand did not forget it, recalling it as an evil omen twenty years later in her novel *Elle et Lui*.

Musset's brother Paul, according to his own *Lui et Elle*, a reply to George Sand's version of her love affair, had dark presentiments too. He remembered how George Sand had abandoned Jules Sandeau. 'Remember,' he warned Alfred, 'that deadly sand bank at Quillebeuf on the Seine where, above the surface of the stream, black flags flutter from the masts of sunken ships. There is a black flag visible in this woman's life and it marks a hidden reef.'

But, wrote Paul, the charm that drew Musset to George Sand stemmed from a profound and hidden source. 'Men of genius, precisely because they have received the cruel gift of feeling more deeply than others, and of expressing themselves as others cannot, are inspired by the need for trials and suffering. A marvellous instinct allows them to distinguish at first sight the beings from whom they can expect great joys and great unhappiness. A fatal and irresistible attraction draws them; the more evident the danger is the more they seek it and the more they bare their hearts to those who will tear them to pieces.'

In December George Sand and Musset set off on their ill-fated journey to Venice. Both of them longed to see Italy; George Sand hoped to find a cure there for the rheumatism that had plagued her that year. She packed Solange off to the country to stay with her husband, arranged for her mother to take Maurice out from school, and, most difficult of all, persuaded Musset's mother, who was strongly opposed to it, to give her consent to the journey. Musset was a devoted and obedient son.

On a grey and foggy evening they boarded the coach to Lyon, on the first stage of their travels. Musset's brother saw them off, noting superstitiously that the number of their coach was thirteen. The lovers laughed at omens. They travelled by river from Lyon to Avignon, their journey enlivened by the company of Stendhal, who was on his way to take up the post of consul in Cività Vecchia. From Marseilles they took the boat to Genoa. They landed in Italy on December 20th, arriving in Venice, after an interlude in Florence, on the last day of the year.

8

1834

'Alfred was a terrible flirt and George did not behave as a perfect gentleman': the epigram on the most publicised of all romantic love affairs was Swinburne's. The journey to Italy had begun in an aura of scandal. Both lovers were famous figures. George Sand was obliged, so she told Sainte-Beuve, to live her private life in public—a fact that did nothing to hinder the sale of her books.

Musset wrote to his family from each stage of their journey, from Genoa, from Florence, where his reading of the old chronicles of the city provided material for his play *Lorenzaccio*, finally from Venice where he described with delight their room at the Danieli hotel and its view across the entrance of the Grand Canal to Santa Maria Salute. Then in February his letters stopped completely. For six weeks his family waited anxiously for news. Paul, his brother, and his mother had decided to set out to Venice in search of him when a letter arrived from Musset announcing his intention to return to Paris as soon as he had sufficient strength. 'I will be bringing home,' he wrote, 'a sick body, a broken spirit, and a heart that is bleeding but which loves you still.'

What had happened? The stay in Venice had started badly. George Sand had fallen unromantically ill from dysentery. Musset was more vexed than sympathetic. 'It's very disagreeable,' he told her, 'to have a sick woman for a companion.' He was irritated too by her perpetual industry, for even though she had taken to her bed she continued to write—the advance for her next novel was paying most of their expenses. Left to his own devices, he fell back on his old habits of dissipation, returning late and sometimes not till dawn, drunk, wild-eyed, once with a bleeding head from some tavern brawl, to where she lay sick and miserable, but too doggedly proud to reproach him. He called her religious, stupid, ennui personified; and one evening, in the casino of the Danieli, he announced to her: 'George, I have made a mistake. I am very sorry but I do not love you.' That evening the door between their two rooms was closed.

George Sand had scarcely recovered when Musset himself fell ill and far more dangerously, with a species of brain fever. For two weeks his life and his reason were in danger; he was often delirious, behaving at times like a madman, flinging himself round the room naked, scream-ing, recoiling from imaginary spirits. All George Sand's maternal instincts rose to the crisis. She nursed him devotedly day and night with the help of a young Italian doctor, Pietro Pagello. Pagello was blonde, fresh-faced, twenty-six years old, a reassuring presence in the midst of her anxiety and exhaustion. Was it in his delirium or was it in reality that Musset saw her sitting on his knee? Was it true, or was it only his imagination that she and the doctor had drunk out of the same cup? By the time that his fever had left him, thanks to their unceasing care, the situation, though both took pains to hide it from him, had been resolved. George Sand had become the mistress of Pagello. It was Musset's turn to suffer, his love reviving with the pangs of jealousy and suspicion.

Musset had told George Sand that he no longer loved her. By George Sand's code of morality he had abandoned his claims to her; there was therefore no treachery in her new liaison. How she master-minded a scene in which Pagello announced to Musset his love for her, how Musset, in a gesture of noble resignation, joined their hands together and swore eternal friendship to them both, is a theme worthy of her novels. On March 29th, in the company of a valet whom George Sand had procured for him, Musset set off back to Paris.

Alone with Pagello and rested after the exhausting ordeal of Musset's illness, George Sand found her new relationship beginning to pall. Pagello was good-natured but prosaic. Distance lent increasing enchantment to her love for Musset and his for her. She had said goodbye to him with a chaste and motherly embrace. Almost as soon as he had departed their passionate duet began again.

'I am still in love with you, George', he wrote from Geneva. 'In four days there will be three hundred miles between us, so why should I not speak frankly? At such a distance there are no more violent emotions or nervous crises; I love you, I know you are with a man that you love, and yet I am calm. The tears are dropping fast as I write to you but they are the sweetest, most precious tears that I have yet shed . . .

'This morning I was wandering through the streets of Geneva, looking at the shops . . . I saw myself reflected in a window and I recognised the child of former times. What did you do, my poor friend? Was this the man you chose to love? You carried ten years of suffering in your heart, for ten years you thirsted for happiness, and this was the reed on which you decided to lean! *You*, love *me*! My poor George! It made me tremble! I made you so unhappy, and I do not know what further unhappiness I was about to cause you. I shall long see your face, my George, pale with eighteen days of watching by my bed; I shall long see you in that ill-omened room where so many tears were shed. Poor George! Poor dear girl! You were mistaken; you thought you were my mistress and you were only my mother . . .'

'Whether I was your mistress or your mother,' George Sand wrote back, 'matters little. Whether I inspired you with love or friendship, whether I was happy or unhappy with you, changes none of my feelings for you. I know that I love you and that is all . . . Why should I, who would have given all my blood to give you a night of peace and rest, have become a torment, a calamity, a spectre to you? Why do these awful memories assail me—and never leave me in peace? I am almost going mad. My pillow is wet with tears. I hear you crying in the night.'

Musset arrived in Paris where he collapsed once more. It was several weeks before he was well enough to leave his rooms and try to recover his former zest for life in the salons of the *noble faubourg*. It was no use, he wrote to George, 'the more I go out the more attached I become to you and, though very calm, I am devoured by an unhappiness that will not leave me'. The letters went back and forth, exalted generalities of love interspersed with practical requests from George—would Musset correct the proofs of her latest novel; would he pursue her editor, Buloz, who had failed to forward the money he owed her to Venice; would he send her twelve pairs of gloves, four pairs of shoes, some patchouli, a packet of press cuttings on her novels which she hoped to have translated in Italy; would he go to see her son Maurice at school? Musset, usually so insouciant, carried out her requests punctiliously and in the midst of the gossip and conjecture which his return from Venice had aroused refused to hear a word against his former mistress. Meanwhile the Italian episode was beginning to bear fruit in literary terms: on George's side with two novels, *Jacques* and *André*, and a series of letters on Italy published in the *Revue des Deux Mondes*, on Musset's with two plays, *Lorenzaccio* and the exquisite tragi-comedy *On ne badine pas avec l'amour*. He was planning too a novel which would commemorate their love: *La Confession d'un Enfant du Siècle*. 'I want to write our story,' he wrote to her; '. . . I want to build you an altar, even though it be with my bones.'

In August, belatedly anxious about her two children, whom she had not seen for eight months, George Sand returned to Paris, bringing Pagello in her wake. Almost immediately there was a harrowing scene with Musset, who, bidding her an eternal farewell, borrowed money from his mother to go to Baden-Baden in an attempt to forget her or die. Poor Pagello was unable to compete at this level of sublimity: bemused and at a disadvantage, he found himself increasingly ignored. 'I perceived with sorrow,' he wrote, 'that she was an actress well accustomed to this sort of farce and the blindfold over my eyes became transparent.' At the end of October, after an unsatisfactory two months spent visiting hospitals in Paris, Pagello returned to Venice, his *amour-propre* and his financial situation considerably restored by the sale of four Venetian paintings he had brought with him, for which George Sand, always generous to departing lovers, had contrived to obtain the sum of twenty thousand francs. His famous romance thereafter assured him a certain celebrity with visitors to Venice and he basked in its glow for the rest of his life. As for George Sand, no sooner had Pagello been dismissed than she flung herself once more into the arms of Musset who had returned from Baden-Baden determined to repossess her. It was soon clear that there would be no happiness in their reunion. 'The greatest thunderstorms I know of,' wrote Sainte-Beuve to a friend in November, 'are the ruptures of Lélia and Rolla, who have spent all this last month in denouncing one another, in being reunited, in tearing each other apart, and in suffering.'

*   *   *

While George Sand and Musset were acting out their drama in full consciousness of the public gaze, two lesser players, equally inspired by the spirit of the age, were involved in another ill-starred love affair: Marie Dorval's eldest daughter, Gabrielle, and the poet Antoine Fontaney. It is time to meet Fontaney whose journal, filled with un-posed glimpses of the great, is one of the most fascinating records of the period. A poet of minor talent but charm and sensibility, he had been a member of the Cénacle in its early days, a habitué of Hugo's salon and the Arsenal, and later one of the circle round Marie Dorval. The actress herself had shown signs of interest in him, to the evident displeasure of Vigny, but it was her daughter Gabrielle, fresh from a convent, whom he sought at her apartment, where their love developed to the accompaniment of snatched kisses in the dining-room and fleet-ing conversations constantly interrupted by other guests, by Gabrielle's jealous younger sister, by the old and grumbling maid. In 1833, nominated to a diplomatic post in Spain, Fontaney left France for a year. Marie Dorval, who hoped to see the intrigue die a natural death with absence, for Fontaney was penniless and his interesting pallor, however fashionable, boded ill for his health, sent Gabrielle back to her convent to forget him. But Gabrielle did not forget him, the two corresponded daily, in passionate terms, and in the spring of 1834, having returned to Paris and being faced with the determined opposition of her mother, Fontaney eloped with Gabrielle to England.

'They left for England,' wrote George Sand, to whom Marie Dorval confided her miseries as a mother, 'thus devouring, at one bite, the little they possessed. Did they hope to find employment in London? Their hopes were not realised. Gabrielle was not an artist though she had been brought up like an heiress, surrounded and advised by true artists;

but beauty without courage or intelligence is not enough. Fontaney was no better endowed; he was a nice young man with an interesting face, capable of kind and tender sentiments but extremely short of ideas . . .'

The two great women, each supreme exponents of romantic passion in their art and in their lives, both deplored its effects in the life of Gabrielle, whom Fontaney, pleading reasons of poverty and difficulty with papers, refused to make his wife. 'Oh, it is odious! It is an eternal sorrow to me,' wrote Marie Dorval to Vigny. '. . . Why did she not preserve her young girl's pride and innocence of heart?' In the romantic canon, indeed in that of the nineteenth century, an unhappy marriage was a necessary pre-condition to taking a lover.

In the midst of this family crisis Marie Dorval had at last made her entry into the Théâtre Français, thanks to the combined efforts of Vigny, Dumas and Hugo, her contract stipulating that she should make her début in *Antony*. Her acceptance was greeted with sullen hostility by the other actors. While she was rehearsing the play and the posters were being put up—delighted, she toured Paris in a cab to look at them —a cabal was being formed behind her back. On the day before the first night, a violent attack on *Antony*, and indirectly on herself, was launched in the *Constitutionnel*, the leading conservative journal: 'The Théâtre Français must not . . . stoop to these grotesque and immoral displays which are a disgrace to our age, an affront to morality, and a mortal danger to society . . . An attempt is being made to foist the actors of the Porte-Saint-Martin onto the Théâtre Français and to naturalise absurd and filthy melodramas there . . . A romantic coterie is seeking to dishonour the stage.' The *Constitutionnel* was powerful, and the Minister of the Interior, yielding to political pressure, agreed to ban the play. Dumas, protesting loudly, received compensation for his loss of receipts, but Marie Dorval, deprived of her chance to re-create her most successful role, found herself condemned to a season of second-rate parts. More and more she looked to Vigny to provide her with a part which would be worthy of her talents, in which she could confound her enemies.

Vigny's life was divided between the bedside of his mother, whom he had moved into his apartment, and that of his wife. The extra expenses caused by his mother's illness involved him in a perpetual struggle to make ends meet. Her outbursts of irrational rage, sometimes falling on the gentle Lydia, sometimes on those looking after her, obliged him to use all his tact in soothing the people she offended. 'I am living on a powder barrel,' he wrote, and again: 'Devotion to another is a folly— a sublime folly, but a folly nonetheless.'

Only at night could he find time to work and think. It was in the silence of the small hours, during seventeen nights of concentrated emotion, his feelings so intense that at times he actually fainted, that he began and completed the play which Marie Dorval, with tears and threats, had begged him to write for her. The play was *Chatterton*— Vigny's greatest theatrical success, with *Hernani* and *Antony* one of the three great landmarks in the French romantic theatre.

It was not at first seen in this light by the committee of the Théâtre Français, who were unanimous in rejecting it at its first reading. It was only through the intervention of the king's son, the Duc d'Orléans, who was sympathetic to Vigny and his work, that it was accepted. The question of casting presented further difficulties, and another royal *démarche*, this time by the king, was required before Marie Dorval rather than Mademoiselle Mars was confirmed in the role of the heroine Kitty Bell. If the pale and ardent figure of Chatterton, worn by nights of thought and watching, expressed Vigny's own sense of spiritual isolation, that of Kitty Bell, trembling before the recognition of her feeling for him, timid, sensitive, expansive only in her devotion to two small children, reflected a vision of Marie Dorval to which, however removed from it in real life, she corresponded to perfection on the stage. Her moment and her justification would come on the first night, early in the following year. In the meantime, conscious of the animosity round her at rehearsals, she reserved her forces, keeping her greatest effects to be judged, not by her fellow players, who despised her as an actress of the boulevards, but by the public who adored her.

*   *   *

On the envelope containing his letters from Victor Hugo is written in Sainte-Beuve's writing: 'He played a double game. He wrote magnificently to me and acted against me. I knew it. Hence for years the hidden duel between us.'

The hidden duel was coming to an end. There was a brief passage of arms in February. Hugo had written a study of Mirabeau in which, indirectly, he sought to explain himself. Mirabeau, like himself, had been a great man subjected to violent and unjust criticism. It was true that at that period Hugo was a much hated figure. Most of his former friends, bruised by his arrogance and egotism, had deserted him; the critics, on all sides, had manhandled him. In a review Sainte-Beuve, affecting astonishment at his treatment, praised his resilience, but, as indirectly as Hugo had written his own defence, attacked him for his too subjective view of what constituted greatness. Hugo recognised the claw beneath the velvet touch of his friend: 'I found in your article (and there are *two* of us who received this impression) great praise, magnificent phrases, but in the end, and this saddens me profoundly, no good will . . . Victor Hugo is overwhelmed, Victor Hugo is grateful, but Victor, your old friend Victor, is grieved.'

Sainte-Beuve wrote back, disclaiming all unfriendly intentions in his article and re-affirming his faith in their relationship, 'to which I have owed and continue to owe so much happiness, and which, after all, is my first claim to fame in the world of letters, just as it was the first overwhelming feeling in my life'.

Two months later came the break that put paid, once and for all, to their increasingly hollow protestations. The immediate cause is unknown, and Sainte-Beuve's letter leading up to it is missing. Hugo's answer was dignified and sad:

'There is so much hatred and cowardly persecution to share with me at present that I perfectly understand why my friends, even the most tried and trusted, should renounce me and cut loose from me. Goodbye then, my friend. Let us each bury in silence that which was already dead in you, and which your letter has killed in me.'

Matters did not end on this high level. A final letter from Sainte-Beuve, enigmatic because the incident it refers to is unknown, closed their correspondence:

'I owe it to my good faith to say that I do not at all accept the interpretation you put upon my last letter. I know what to believe or not to believe of the conversation which was reported to me; another person, besides the one who was in the apartment with you, heard it, the door being thinner and your voice louder than you thought. Let us leave it at that, I beg you. It's ascribing too much importance, not, as you suggest, to unworthy people, but to an unworthy subject. Continue to write your lovely poems and I shall try to write conscientious articles; return to your work as I shall to my profession. I have no temple and despise no one. You have a temple; see to it that it remains untouched by scandal.'

With this reference to Juliette, the friendship ended, dead beyond resurrection though outward relations between the two continued, for a time, to be amicable. Hugo was still not aware of the extent of Sainte-Beuve's treachery, of the assignations with Adèle or of the correspondence between them; intensely in love as he now was with Juliette Drouet, perhaps he would no longer have cared.

Adèle Hugo, her position made easier by her essential indifference, had put a good face on Hugo's infidelity; it had, at the least, put an end to his physical demands. By common accord they continued to present a united front as a family to the world, Adèle, unexpectedly, taking an increasing pleasure in her role as hostess in the splendid salon in the Place Royale and as the wife of a great man.

'I do not want to say anything that would make you sad while you

are away, being unable to be near you to console you,' she wrote to
Hugo that summer while he was travelling in Brittany with Juliette
Drouet. 'And besides I am sure that you love me at heart and that you
are enjoying yourself since you are so slow in returning: and in truth
these two certainties make me happy.'

Hugo's 'Date Lilia', written on his return to his family in September,
was a hymn of gratitude to his wife:

> Oh! si vous rencontrez quelque part, sous les cieux
> Une femme au front pur, au pas grave, aux doux yeux,
> Que suivent quatre enfants dont le dernier chancelle . . .
> Oh! qui que vous soyez, bénissez-la. C'est elle!
> La soeur, visible aux yeux, de mon âme immortelle!
> Mon orgeuil, mon espoir, mon abri, mon recours!
> Toit de mes jeunes ans qu'espèrent mes vieux jours! . . .

The Hugos were once more staying with their friends the Bertins at
Bièvre. The little church where, in a previous year, Adèle had secretly
met Sainte-Beuve, was the setting for one of Hugo's loveliest poems to
Juliette Drouet whom he had installed in a house at Metz near by and
whom he met almost daily in the woods.

> C'était une humble église, au cintre surbaissé,
> L'église où nous entrâmes,
> Où depuis trois cent ans avaient déjà passé
> Et pleuré bien des âmes.
>
> Elle était triste et calme à la chute du jour,
> L'église où nous entrâmes;
> L'autel sans serviteur, comme un coeur sans amour
> Avait éteint ses flammes . . .

After the storms and scenes of the last year, Juliette had taken the
plunge of breaking with her protector Prince Demidoff and the life of
luxury with which he had surrounded her, trusting from now on to
Hugo and her hopes of success as an actress. The financial consequences
were appalling. Juliette was left with debts so enormous that at first she
dared not reveal them to her lover. No further theatrical engagements
had been forthcoming since her failure in *Marie Tudor*. She tried vainly
to borrow from friends, she pawned the major part of her wardrobe—
the items, jewellery apart, included thirty-eight dresses, forty-four
peignoirs, eighty-four cambric chemises and thirty-one embroidered
petticoats. She moved from the sumptuous apartment in which she had

been maintained by Demidoff to a little two-room flat in the Rue Paradis-des-Marais. Nonetheless, early in August, brought to bay by the unassuaged demands of her creditors, she was forced to reveal the total amount of her debts—the horrifying sum of twenty thousand francs. Hugo, who even as a young man, living close to starvation on a few sous a day, had been too proud to borrow, reacted violently, his fury aroused equally by the amount of the debt and the past it conjured up. Juliette, shattered and despairing, fled with her daughter to Brittany and it was there, while Adèle Hugo was writing her letter of indulgence to her absent husband, that Hugo caught up with her and the lovers made their peace, Hugo swearing, cost what it might, to work to pay off her debts one by one, Juliette, who had sacrificed everything for his sake, acquiescing in an existence that would henceforth be one of near poverty. Their travels in Brittany, and their sojourn in the valley of Bièvre thereafter, were filled with idyllic happiness but there were moments of sadness too, for Juliette. Hugo, magnificent in his resolution to save her, just as Marion de Lorme, the courtesan, had been redeemed by love, did not always spare her his reproaches for the past. In the little church at Bièvre where she knelt with bowed head, she wept, crushed by doubt and discouragement. Hugo's poem, written for her on the evening of that day, captured the emotion of the moment in verses of timeless beauty, but the consolation he had to offer to poor Juliette, humiliated by her earlier life, was a sad one:

> O madame! pourquoi ce chagrin qui vous suit?
> Pourquoi pleurer encore,
> Vous, femme au coeur charmant, sombre comme la
>   nuit,
> Douce comme l'aurore?
>
> Qu'importe que la vie, inégale ici-bas
> Pour l'homme et pour la femme,
> Se dérobe et soit prête à rompre sous vos pas?
> N'avez-vous pas votre âme?
>
> Votre âme qui bientôt fuira peut-être ailleurs
> Vers les régions pures,
> Et vous emportera plus loin que nos douleurs,
> Plus loin que nos murmures!
>
> Soyez comme l'oiseau, posé pour un instant
> Sur des rameaux trop frêles,
> Qui sent ployer la branche et qui chante pourtant,
> Sachant qu'il a des ailes!

*   *   *

'My dear friend,' wrote Alfred de Musset to his friend Alfred Tattet in mid-November, 'everything is finished. If by any chance someone [George Sand] asks you questions (since it's possible that you will be suspected of having spoken to me) or indeed comes to ask you if you've seen me, simply answer no . . .'

Alfred Tattet was Musset's closest friend. He had visited the lovers in Venice where he had shared George Sand's anxieties during Musset's illness. 'If anyone asks you what you think of the ferocious Lélia', she had written to him after his visit, 'tell them that she does not live on the waters of the sea and the blood of men, in which she is very much inferior to Han d'Islande; tell them that she lives on boiled chicken, that she wears slippers in the morning and that she smokes Maryland cigarettes. And for yourself alone, remember that you have seen her suffer and be sorry for herself, like any normal person.'

But Alfred Tattet, like Musset's other friends, had grown to deplore the influence of the ferocious Lélia, seeing its effects on Musset's shattered nerves and dangerous state of exaltation. During Pagello's stay in Paris, Tattet, who had been kind to him for Musset's sake, had received his complaints and confidences about George, including the fact that, contrary to what she had led Musset to believe when with a noble gesture he had confided her to Pagello, she had already been Pagello's mistress for some weeks. It was this revelation and the fury of Musset's retrospective jealousy that had completed the rupture between them.

George Sand, more deeply in love than she had been at any other stage of their relationship, was in despair. She attempted vainly to see Musset, she bought a death's head in which to keep his final letter to her and then, passion and wounded vanity driving her to further romantic gestures, cut off her long black hair and sent it to him. Delacroix's painting of her, for which she sat that November, records her appearance, her hair cut jaggedly short, her vast eyes dark with unhappiness. From friends like Sainte-Beuve she sought comfort and advice. Sainte-Beuve advised her to seek distraction in study and conversation, and Liszt told her that only God deserved to be loved. 'That may be,' George wrote in her journal, 'but when one has loved a man it is difficult to love God, it's so very different.'

She took herself to the theatre, dressed in her usual boyish garb, and compared herself, lonely and demoralised, to the pretty women in the circle, blonde, bare-shouldered, with their pink and white complexions, their curls, their plumes and their bouquets. 'And where am I, poor George?' she sighed. 'See, up above me, the fields where Fantasio plucks his flowers.' Her misery gathered momentum; her journal, written over this period, rises to a crescendo of regret and anguish. She had been betrayed both by Pagello and Musset and their 'miserable masculine *amour-propre*'. How could she have told Musset of her relations with Pagello, while he was still ill? He would have died of anger if she had not lied to him, and later, if she had not continued to lie, he would have died of sorrow. She contemplated killing herself, torturing herself as she imagined the feelings of her orphaned children, of her son returning alone down the cold corridors of his school after his mother's death had been announced to him by a stranger. 'Oh my son! my son. I pray that you may read this one day, and know how much I've loved you. Tears, tears of my heart, sign this page, and may his own tears one day find your traces after his name.'

And then, in mid-December, came an abatement of her miseries. 'My excellent friend,' she wrote to Sainte-Beuve, announcing this surcease, 'I should have written to you sooner but I'm sure that you'll understand that it has taken me some days to recover myself and to realise to what a pass that dreadful nightmare had led me . . .

'Alfred has written me an affectionate letter, repenting deeply of his violence towards me. His heart is so good, in spite of everything. I have sent him, as my only answer, a little leaf from my garden, and he has sent me a lock of his hair, for which I have long been begging him, that is to say for the last fortnight; and there we are, it's all over. I no longer wish to see him again, it would hurt me too much.'

9

1835

Alfred Tattet, in George Sand's eyes, had been the cause of her break-up with Musset. Pagello, to do him justice, had never wished his confidences to be repeated to Musset and had left conjuring Tattet to secrecy. Throughout the period following Tattet's revelation, Tattet had done his best to prevent a reconciliation. So it must have been with satisfaction that on January 14th, 1835 George Sand was able to write to him:

'Monsieur—there are certain surgical operations which are extremely well performed and do honour to the skill of the surgeon but which do not prevent the illness from recurring. Such a recurrence was always a possibility. Alfred has once more become my lover.'

The lovers were re-united, but not for long. Musset found new causes for jealousy in George Sand's friendships, with Liszt, with Marie Dorval; George Sand, sober, professional, was appalled by Musset's bouts of drunkenness and the cruelty and caprice which alternated with his passionate declarations of love. But only by living through this final round were the lovers at last able to let go. 'No, no,' wrote George Sand to Musset in early March, 'it is enough! Poor unhappy one, I loved you like a son, it was a mother's love I had for you . . . I can struggle no longer. God has made me gentle but also proud. My pride is bruised and bleeding now; my love is no longer anything but pity. I tell you, we must get over this. Sainte-Beuve is right. Your conduct is deplorable, impossible. My God, what kind of life am I leaving you to! Drunkenness, wine, women, now and forever more. But since I can do nothing to save you, there is no longer any point in prolonging what only brings shame to me and torment to you. My tears irritate you. And then in the midst of it all comes your mad jealousy flaring at nothing. The less right you have to be jealous, the more jealous you become. It seems like God's judgement on your poor head.'

She left Paris for Nohant, her country estate, without saying goodbye.

*   *   *

The Sand-Musset drama had its public as well as its private side. George Sand's re-possession of Musset would not have been complete, or her wounded pride restored, without the demonstration of her victory to the world. Together in February they had attended Vigny's *Chatterton*.

'My friend,' wrote George Sand to Marie Dorval next morning, 'I must tell you that I have never seen you so beautiful, so intelligent and so admirable as yesterday evening. The play is extremely beautiful, touching, exquisite in its sentiment. I came out in tears, unable to say a word to anyone because I was incapable of speech . . . Only a noble heart and an exceptional spirit could produce such a work. I do not at all like the person of M. de Vigny; in which I do not resemble you (that's very witty, isn't it?), but I assure you that on the level of one soul to another I esteem him otherwise. Make him happy, my child; such men have need of happiness and deserve it.'

The first night of *Chatterton* had been a triumph beyond everything Vigny could have hoped. He had seen, with something like disdain, the successes of Hugo and Dumas. 'It is with the commonplace side of one's talent that one succeeds in the theatre, just as in politics it is vulgar qualities that make one popular,' he had written in his journal. '. . . I only seek to show the choicest of my thoughts: I will never be popular.'

And now, as he watched through a hole in the décor, he observed the audience throughout the performance 'as one watches an enemy in a duel, observing the effects of one's blows to his heart and those to his head as well'. The queen and the royal princes were in the dress circle with the established lions of the literary, political and social worlds, but the parterre was crowded with Chatterton's spiritual comrades—pale young men, wrote Théophile Gautier, who was among them, whose burning eyes proclaimed their belief that art and poetry were the only possible occupations on earth.

Profound attention was Vigny's first reward from the audience. After the tirades, swashbuckling, intrigues and coincidences of romantic drama, the absolute simplicity of *Chatterton*, in which external action was reduced to a minimum and silence at times was as expressive as words, evoked a corresponding stillness from the normally volatile Parisians. Balzac summed up the plot derisively: 'First act: should I kill myself? Second act: I should kill myself. Third act: I do kill myself.'

'I wished to demonstrate', wrote Vigny in the preface to his play, 'how the spiritual man is stifled by a materialistic society in which the grasping calculator pitilessly exploits intelligence and work.' The story of Chatterton, the seventeen-year-old poet whose suicide in a garret had already formed an episode in his *Stello*, was the vehicle for his plea for the creative artist at odds with an uncomprehending world.

'They are about to play *Chatterton*,' he had noted at six o'clock that evening. 'I am writing this standing up. I feel entirely calm, convinced that if the play should not succeed it would be no more than a delay for the inevitable success of spiritual drama.'

At twelve o'clock, with the exaltation of extreme fatigue, he returned to his journal. '*Chatterton* has succeeded,' he wrote. '. . . The public was united like one man on whose face I could progressively read the words:

' "I have confidence in you, I know you to be sincere, I am listening. Speak."

'And then, "I am moved by what you say, your plea for the poet is just."

'And then, "I feel that you too have suffered this."

'And then, stretching out his arms to me, "I am yours, I love you, I am your friend."

˙ 'It was then that my friends came to me and threw themselves on my neck in floods of tears. They babbled disconnectedly, they cried: "My friend, my friend!" They also had shared the martyrdom I had written about.

'My heart was filled with a feeling of gentle sadness, my eyes filled with tears despite myself. I thought of the unhappiness that is caused by too great a distrust of one's brothers. I felt remorse at having misjudged my fellow citizens . . .'

For Marie Dorval, as much as for her lover, *Chatterton* was a vindication and a triumph. In Kitty Bell, speechlessly in love with Chatterton, she found perhaps her greatest role. It was a role in half-tints, according with her modest dress in Quaker grey, in which the passions which she had expressed so vibrantly in other parts remained unspoken. In the final act, when Kitty Bell climbs the stairs to Chatterton's room to find that he has taken poison and is dying, the contrast between the violence of her despair and her painful repression of feeling until that moment was almost unbearable. There was a cry of 'assez' from the audience. 'I leaned motionless against the box,' wrote Maxime du Camp, who was carried out fainting at the end of the performance, 'a prey to feelings I had never experienced before; and I felt as though I were choking.' Marie Dorval had reserved her most sensational effect for the opening night, her *dégringolade*, or dying fall, from the top of the staircase outside Chatterton's room. She had refused to rehearse it or to reveal her plans to her fellow actors who shared the shock and terror of the audience as she fell back over the bannister with an anguished cry and toppled head-first, arms outstretched, from top to bottom of the stairs. 'Ah,' wrote Théophile Gautier, 'if only Chatterton could have opened his opium-laden eyes one last time on such an abandon of grief he would have died happy, sure that he was loved as no man ever was and that it would not be long before he met his sister soul below.'

If Dumas' *Antony* had opened the way for a spate of misunderstood wives and demonic lovers, *Chatterton* gave birth to an equal number of neglected geniuses. The romantic generation had always been in love with death. 'What a marvellous place to kill oneself!' cried Alfred de Musset, when he was confronted with a beautiful view. The cult of suicide reached its apogee with *Chatterton*. 'Those were the days,' wrote Gautier, 'when you could hear the crack of solitary pistol shots in the night.' Vigny was appalled by the play's effects: he had meant to plead the cause of poets, not encourage them to kill themselves. Unwittingly, he found himself cast as the patron of potential Chattertons, a role he would play nobly all his life. 'He made himself the high priest of unhappy youth,' wrote Sainte-Beuve maliciously, but Vigny's mission was more than a pose. Too proud and perhaps too maladroit to intrigue for himself, he could be importunate on behalf of others, stretching his influence and his slender purse for those he considered deserving. In the materialistic days of the Second Empire Flaubert would speak of him as the sole comforting and consoling figure in the world of letters; and it is moving to think of him, already old and stricken with his last illness, befriending Baudelaire whose genius he was among the first to recognise and encourage.

Immediate reactions to *Chatterton*, despite the emotion of the opening night, were not all favourable. Conservative critics condemned it as immoral, seeing in Chatterton's despairing pride an excuse for idleness and self-pity. To these hostile criticisms Alfred de Musset, ever devoted to Vigny, responded with two indignant sonnets, dashed off on his return from a performance. George Sand copied out the first at his dictation:

> Quand vous aurez prouvé, messieurs du journalisme,
> Que Chatterton eut tort de mourir ignoré,
> Qu'au Théâtre Français on l'a défiguré
> Quand vous aurez crié sept fois à l'athéisme,
> Sept fois au contresens et sept fois au sophisme
> Vous n'aurez pas prouvé que je n'ai pas pleuré . . .

Vigny wrote both sonnets proudly in his journal.

*　　*　　*

George Sand had kept copies of both Musset's sonnets, which she had shown to Buloz, the editor of the *Revue des Deux Mondes*. A few days later, Musset, already close to breaking point with her, wrote to Buloz to beg him to burn them, not, he wrote, for any want of admiration for Vigny or his play but out of literary pride. '*Que voulez-vous, mon cher ami?*

They were verses written in haste; I am a craftsman in verse; it is my profession . . .'

Through all the hectic emotions of the last year and in spite of the drunkenness and dissipation which accompanied them, Musset had retained his seriousness as an artist. The plays of 1833 and 1834, for all their lyricism, are almost classical in their sense of form and in the author's detachment from his subject matter. Only in poetry, the most personal and spontaneous form of expression, had he remained virtually silent.

In the calm after George's departure, he once more felt the sap begin to rise in him. 'Having asked of my sorrow all that it could answer, having drunk and tasted my own tears,' he wrote to Alfred Tattet, 'I have finished by feeling stronger than my grief . . . It seems to me that I shall soon speak and that there is something in my soul that insists on being expressed.'

One evening in May, after a walk under the chestnut trees in the Tuileries Gardens, he recited to his brother the first two stanzas of a dialogue between the poet and his Muse:

> *La Muse:*
> Poète, prends ton luth et me donne un baiser;
> La fleur de l'églantier sent ses bourgeons éclore.
> Le printemps naît ce soir; les vents vont
> s'embraser;
> Et la bergeronnette, en attendant l'aurore,
> Aux premiers buissons verts commence à se poser.
> Poète, prends ton luth, et me donne un baiser.

> *Le Poète:*
> Comme il fait noir dans la vallée!
> J'ai cru qu'une forme voilée
> Flottait là-bas sur le forêt.
> Elle sortait de la prairie;
> Son pied rasait l'herbe fleurie;
> C'est une étrange rêverie;
> Elle s'efface et disparaît.

The poem was 'La Nuit de mai', the first of the great poems to which his sufferings with George Sand gave birth:

> Rien ne nous rend si grands qu'une grande douleur.
> . . . Les plus désespérés sont les chants les plus
> beaux,
> Et j'en sais d'immortels qui sont de purs sanglots.

'La Nuit de mai' was a distillation of Musset's feelings for George Sand. His novel, *La Confession d'un Enfant du Siècle*, which he completed that year, examined them at length, and in doing so gave a brilliant analysis not only of his own dilemmas, but those of his generation, 'conceived between two battles', reaching manhood to face the sense of emptiness and spiritual malaise that followed the fall of the Empire. Brigitte Pierson, the heroine, is represented as altogether virtuous and charming, Octave, the hero, is stricken with the malady of the age. Lacking beliefs, betrayed in his first love, he has plunged into debauchery; the infection of disillusion has entered his blood, and when in Brigitte he finds his ideal woman he ruins their love by his cruelty and infidelity, redeeming himself in the end by the magnanimity with which he withdraws from her to give place to a man more worthy of her love —in other words Pagello.

'I cried like an idiot,' wrote George Sand when she read it. 'And then I wrote a few lines to the author to say I know not what: that I loved him very much, that I had forgiven him, and that I never wished to see him again.'

Musset too had no wish to re-open his wounds save in literary terms. The year had brought forth a rich harvest: two plays, *Le Chandelier* and *La Quenouille de Barberine*, 'La Nuit de décembre' and a handful of shorter poems including 'Lucie' whose famous incantation,

> Mes chers ámis, quand je mourrai
> Plantez un saule au cimitière . . .

would be written on his grave. The attempted assassination of Louis-Philippe and his sons in Paris, in a bomb attack in which forty-eight people had been killed, had woken him temporarily from his personal preoccupations. The incident had dealt the *coup de grâce* to overt republican opposition in France; insurrections in Lyon and Paris, brutally put down in the previous year, had been followed by a mass trial of the insurgents in April. In the wave of shock which followed the assassination attempt the government took the opportunity to pass a law which effectively muzzled all opposition in the press. Musset, stirred from his normal indifference to politics, was moved to protest: his spirited poem 'La Loi sur la Presse' completed the sum of his writings that year. The trial of Fieschi, the assassin, would be the big event of the following spring.

*　　*　　*

In October 1835 Alfred de Vigny published his *Servitude et Grandeur Militaires*, a series of sketches of military life based in part on his own experiences as a soldier and linked by a single idea: the concept of military honour. The soldier, like the poet, belongs to a race apart; he is a 'gladiator, sacrificed to the political fantasies of the sovereign or the people', whose stoical obedience is the source of his greatness as it is of his servitude. '*Cinq-Mars, Stello, Servitude et Grandeur Militaires* (it has been aptly remarked),' wrote Vigny in his journal, 'are the strains of an epic poem of disillusion.' The theme of *Cinq-Mars* had been the destruction of the feudal aristocracy under Richelieu: as an aristocrat, a poet and a soldier Vigny could see himself as a triple outcast.

His private troubles underlined his literary pessimism. The joy which he had felt after the first night of *Chatterton* was short-lived. It had won him neither gratitude nor peace from Marie Dorval. 'It is impossible not to relieve my feelings by complaining of your treatment of me,' he wrote to her in April. 'You are making me very unhappy. I cannot live like this . . . Don't think I have ever deceived myself as to the degree of egoistic calculation and bad feeling in your heart. Everything is devotion on my side; for four years every hour of my days and often of my nights has been spent in seeking how to make you happy, and during all that time you seem to have employed yourself in devising ways to hurt me and inventing new pain for the morrow. The contrast has become too bitter.

'I knew very well last summer, when I was ill, and I saw you crying because things were going so badly for you at the theatre, what a risk I was taking in trying to save you—how many enemies and how few friends I had, and how serious a matter failure would be for me; and yet you took pleasure in hurting and tormenting me . . .

'Ah! I beg you, go no further!

'Do not heap more injuries on me than my love and kindness can bear.'

Marie Dorval counter-attacked. The figure of George Sand had once more come between them, but the jealousy this time was on Marie Dorval's side. Vigny had met George Sand in Marie Dorval's dressing-room, and despite his professed antipathy had offered her his arm to escort her home. Marie Dorval, inhibited by her husband's presence, had been unable to protest.

'I am striving with all my might,' she wrote to him that night, 'to find some wound, some pain, which will cut you to the heart, so that I can pay back the torment of this evening. To have to go home and let you go without vengeance, to have to wait! You are the coldest and most horrible of men, and the wickedest and the clumsiest too. You are incapable of hiding your feelings. You were unable to conceal the pleasure you took in spending the whole evening next to that woman . . . You were enjoying yourself so much, so much! I could say nothing

—anyway it's not you she loves, and I am not angry with her—but you, you took advantage of my situation, you knew that you were hurting me, and you took her with you and she put her hand on your arm, and you will never know the extent of my rage and hatred for you.'

The role of George Sand in the Vigny–Dorval relationship was clearly a complex one, but the violence of Marie Dorval's reproaches may have owed something to a sense of guilt. After only two months, she was in the process of abandoning Vigny's *Chatterton* for a role in Victor Hugo's new play, *Angelo, Tyran de Padoue*.

'An actor takes a role like a dress, puts it on, crumples it, and then throws it away,' Vigny commented in his journal.

*   *   *

Hugo had produced nothing for the theatre in the previous year. In his study of Mirabeau and in a collection of essays he had proclaimed his political convictions and traced his evolution from the royalism of his youth; in a novel, *Claude Gueux*, he had attacked the injustice of a social system weighted against the poor and underprivileged; the theme of *Les Misérables* was already in his mind. But neither novels nor essays brought such a good financial return as plays— *Hernani* had earned four times as much as *Notre-Dame de Paris*. The burden of supporting his own family, and now of Juliette's debts as well, was heavy. *Angelo*, like his previous plays, would bring a welcome addition to his income.

The play was memorable for bringing into confrontation for the first time the leading exponents of two rival traditions: Mademoiselle Mars, icy, aristocratic, steeped in the classical repertoire, and Marie Dorval, the actress of the boulevards, spontaneous, plebeian, with a scandalous past behind her. Mademoiselle Mars, let it be added, had enjoyed the support of rich protectors; Marie Dorval, however freely she had scattered her favours, had never sold herself, maintaining not only her children but her husband by her work.

There were two main female parts in the play, equal in importance. 'Catarina,' wrote Adèle Hugo, 'married and chaste, suited to perfection the straightforward, respectable talent of Mademoiselle Mars; but Tisbe, the woman of the streets, violent and dissolute, seemed made for the free and bohemian talent of Madame Dorval.' To Mademoiselle Mars, as the reigning queen of the Théâtre Français, Hugo offered the choice of roles. She naturally chose that of Tisbe.

Throughout the rehearsals Mademoiselle Mars treated Marie Dorval with the lofty disdain of a great lady forced to associate with a refugee from the boulevards. Her scorn, however, was mixed with fear of the other's talent; she consoled herself with the thought that if the role of

Tisbe suited her ill, that of the pure and dignified Catarina was still less appropriate to Marie Dorval.

Marie Dorval, in contrast to her rival, was supple and caressing in manner, responding to insults with flattery and humbly acknowledging her rashness in setting foot upon the noble boards of the Théâtre Français. She played the part of Catarina flatly and without expression, biding her time, as with *Chatterton*, until the opening night. Mademoiselle Mars was congratulating herself on the success of her calculations when one day Marie Dorval, forgetting herself at rehearsal, showed a glimpse of her real powers.

Mademoiselle Mars, thoroughly alarmed, switched her attack. She complained of the length of Marie Dorval's speeches and advised Hugo to change the manner of Catarina's death—Marie Dorval had been especially touching in the death scene. Hugo refused to alter what he had written, and the next day, at the rehearsal, when Marie Dorval, as the dying Catarina, sank to her knees at her *prie-dieu*, Mademoiselle Mars, whose place had been at the other side of the stage, deliberately crossed over to stand between her and the audience.

This passed all bearing. Hugo insisted that she return to her original position. Mademoiselle Mars refused, and Hugo, as he had at the rehearsals of *Hernani*, issued an ultimatum. He had never seen such a shameless display of envy. Did Mademoiselle Mars imagine she could stifle Marie Dorval, her equal in talent and success, as though she were some poor aspiring débutante? The part would be played as he intended it or not at all. And, declaring the rehearsal at an end, he left the theatre.

There was consternation at the Théâtre Français. A great deal of time and money had already been spent on the production. The unfortunate manager, caught between two such powerful personalities, wrote to Hugo begging him to make some compromise. Marie Dorval herself wrote, advising him if necessary to give in to Mademoiselle Mars. The success of her part did not depend on that scene alone.

But Mademoiselle Mars had learnt her lesson. She appeared next day at rehearsals and without being asked took her proper station in the death scene. She seemed, wrote Madame Hugo, to be much softened, and after the rehearsal invited Hugo to her dressing-room to see her costumes. Hugo blenched at the sight of the head-dress she intended to wear—a creation half way between a turban and a wagon-wheel, which she had already worn for the part of Doña Sol in *Hernani* to the great astonishment of the spectators, and which was now further embellished with a bird of paradise—but dared not renew their differences by criticising it.

*   *   *

The period of rehearsals had been a melancholy time for Juliette Drouet. Through Hugo's influence she had obtained a position in the Comédie Française. It had not been unreasonable for her to hope that one of the two parts in *Angelo* might be offered to her, but the committee of the Théâtre Français had been against it and Hugo himself, despite his praise for her performance in *Marie Tudor*, was secretly unwilling to entrust his play to an actress as yet unproven. Juliette had sensed his hesitation: 'I am afraid that your apparent lack of concern about my dramatic career must be regarded as a formal statement that I cannot aspire to a future in my art,' she wrote to him sadly. The casting of *Angelo* spelled the end of her hopes and she withdrew from the Théâtre Français without ever having played a role.

Alone in her little flat, living on the merest shoestring, her every expenditure closely watched by Hugo, she allowed herself from time to time a cry of complaint. Hugo was working, busy at home or with rehearsals, and sometimes did not come to see her for several days. In a letter to him, the last lines of which were smudged with tears, she described how she stood for an hour outside his home one evening, seeing the light shining in his dining-room but not daring to ask if he was in. Hugo's championship of Marie Dorval caused her profound uneasiness. 'I am jealous of a woman of flesh and blood', she wrote, 'with the most lustful temperament imaginable, who is there every day, talking to you, looking at you, touching you! Oh yes, I am jealous of her! The suffering it causes me is frightful.'*

The first night of *Angelo*, with its promised confrontation, brought crowds to the theatre. Mademoiselle Mars, having tried and failed to have Marie Dorval's name printed in smaller type than her own on the play-bills, had at last resigned herself to her rival's popularity and concentrated on ensuring her own. Both had their following in the audience: for Mademoiselle Mars the aristocrats and prosperous bourgeoisie, for Marie Dorval the young bohemians who had wept at *Chatterton*. But it was Marie Dorval, not Mademoiselle Mars, who carried the evening and ensured its success.

'If you knew with what sincerity I applauded Madame Dorval,' wrote Juliette Drouet to Hugo on returning from the first performance, 'you would make it a point of honour to say or do nothing which could wound my poor heart, already saddened that someone other than myself is permitted to interpret your noblest thoughts.'

* An intriguing footnote to Juliette's attitude lies in a letter from the critic Gustave Planche to George Sand two years before: 'One of my friends, who from the intimacy of his relations with Juliette Drouet has every reason to believe the truth of her story, assures me that Marie Dorval had a passion for her of the same nature that Sappho had for the young Lesbians.'

She found compensation for her frustrated aspirations not only in the flow of marvellous poetry addressed to her that year but in a summer holiday together, spent first in a month of carefree travelling, and then in the valley of Bièvre, where Hugo would leave ·his family each day to meet her in the woods near Metz. Hugo's lines, written for her that summer, would be engraved upon her tomb:

> Quand je ne serai plus qu'une cendre glacée,
> Quand mes yeux fatigués seront fermés au jour,
> Dis-toi, si dans ton coeur ma mémoire est fixée:
> Le Monde a sa pensée,
> Moi j'avais son amour!

* * *

At the end of July, Adèle Hugo, accompanied by her father and her daughter Léopoldine, travelled to Angers to attend the marriage of their friend Victor Pavie. 'I am sending your young wife my best and sweetest possessions,' Hugo wrote to Pavie, 'my wife and daughter, my two angels.' He himself remained behind, free to travel with Juliette.

Sainte-Beuve too attended the wedding and the celebrations that followed it—lunch for fifty in a tent, a supper party in the open air. His conversation, Pavie's brother recalled, sparkled with wit and poetry at the supper. Adèle, still beautiful with her distinguished features and thick black hair, was laughing and relaxed. 'Poor Adèle,' writes Sainte-Beuve's biographer André Billy, 'she so seldom had a chance to laugh at Place Royale.'

During the three days between the wedding party and the *retour de noces*, when the celebrations were rounded off with a final dinner (at which Sainte-Beuve read a long and laborious epithalamium), Adèle, with her father and daughter, travelled down the river by steamer as far as Nantes, Sainte-Beuve full of solicitude and respectful attentions on their journey. 'When you are in Paris,' wrote Adèle to her husband, who was touring in Normandy with Juliette, 'do write him a little line of thanks for his kindness to us.'

Adèle's letter made two things clear, first that she no longer feared Hugo's suspicion of Sainte-Beuve, secondly that despite the formal cessation of their friendship, relations between the two men were relatively cordial. This state of affairs was soon to come to an end.

In October 1835 Hugo published a new collection of poems, *Les Chants du Crépuscule*. For the first time Sainte-Beuve had not been asked to a preliminary reading but he was pretty well aware what they would be like. 'We're going to have a lyrical volume from Hugo in a fortnight,' he wrote to a friend; 'there will be poems of love; despite all sorts of hesitations he's decided to go ahead regardless, and though it'll be one unity more that he's broken in his poetic life (domestic unity after political and religious) it matters little to us other defiers of the unities, and even less to the public; fine verses, as I'm sure his will be, will cloak and glorify his sin.'

A great number of the poems in *Les Chants du Crépuscule* were indeed poems of love, addressed more or less overtly to Juliette Drouet, but the volume closed with three poems dedicated to Adèle, culminating with his 'Date Lilia'.

'There's a great deal on the fair Delilah,' wrote Sainte-Beuve in another letter. 'He accommodates it all as best he can, *à la chinoise*, with the conjugal love of *Les Feuilles d'Automne* which he does not wish to break with officially.'

Such private comments would have meant little to Hugo, but his anger knew no bounds when in a review in the *Revue des Deux Mondes* he found himself publicly berated for his lack of taste in combining 'two colours that clash, two incenses that repel one another', in the same volume of poems. In finishing the collection with 'Date Lilia', wrote Sainte-Beuve, 'one might almost say that the author is attempting to throw a handful of lilies in our eyes'.

Hugo threatened to challenge Sainte-Beuve to a duel and was only dissuaded by his wife and his editor. Sainte-Beuve was unrepentant, armoured in virtuous indignation: Hugo's immorality was shameful; he would willingly strike him across the face. But he found no support from Adèle Hugo, who from this moment would gradually withdraw from him, and he recognised that with this article the break with Hugo was irrevocable.

'My relations with Hugo were henceforward perfectly simple,' he wrote in his *Cahiers*. 'They come down to this: underneath we were enemies, mortal enemies; in deference to others and ourselves we had only to preserve the conventions of good manners. As for his works, my judgement remains unchanged: as for his lyric poetry, no one could ever express greater admiration than I; as for his dramatic work, no one could ever say worse of it than I think.'

And elsewhere in his *Cahiers*, returning to the subject, as he would again and again:

'You are very great, no doubt, Monsieur, but the world is even greater. It is large enough, believe me, for one to live in it and to avoid you, for one to travel far, and never meet you, for you to imagine that you fill it, and yet for one not to know you and to feel free to forget you.'

But the shadow of Hugo was too vast, the place he had filled in his heart too great, for Sainte-Beuve ever to do this.

10

1836

In 1836 romantic drama, 'that great monster', as Thackeray described it disrespectfully in his *Paris Sketch Book*, 'which has sprung into life of recent years and is said, though I don't believe a word of it, to have Shakespeare for a father', showed signs of losing ground. The public were growing impatient of its extravagances; soberer tastes, more suited to the reign of the citizen king, were beginning to prevail. At the Théâtre Français the classical faction, long in retreat, began at last to hope for a return to the values so rudely overthrown. They would see the fulfilment of their hopes with the advent, two years later, of the young Jewish actress Rachel, who would bring new life to Racine and Corneille; meanwhile, they drew comfort from the revival in popularity of the neo-classical tragedies of Casimir Delavigne, a dramatist for some time eclipsed by the romantics and now drawing nightly crowds to his plays.

The Porte-Saint-Martin, scene of so many romantic triumphs, was foundering into bankruptcy and attempts to revive its fortunes with acts starring elephants and tigers could only lower its literary prestige. Its best writers in any case had deserted it. Hugo, having quarrelled with Harel, would write for it no longer. Vigny, brooding over the ingratitude of Marie Dorval, had abandoned the theatre altogether. Only Dumas remained willing to provide new works and he was inspired above all by the need to make money quickly. His debts and his extravagances were only matched by his generosity. 'I have never refused money to anyone,' he said, 'except to my creditors.'

Dumas had returned from six months spent travelling in Italy and Switzerland with great plans and, it was said, with five new plays. The first of these, *Don Juan da Marana* was produced at the Porte-Saint-Martin that spring. A quasi-religious fantasy, it was variously set, according to Thackeray, 'in heaven (where we have the Virgin Mary with little angels in blue swinging censers before her!), on earth, under the earth, and in a place still lower, not mentionable to ears polite'. Harel, a circus director at heart, spent lavishly on spectacular stage effects. Ida Ferrier, cast in the double role of Don Juan's good angel (to whom he seldom listened) and his mistress, went mad for love in the manner of Ophelia, but Don Juan's chief victims, said the critics, were the authors whose works had been pillaged by Dumas. The play was an expensive failure. 'Dumas has gone down ceremoniously with all flags flying,' wrote Sainte-Beuve to a friend. 'I doubt if he will rise again.'

The ebullient Dumas could not be sunk so easily. His second play that year, *Kean ou Désordre et Génie*, was a brilliant success. Dumas had written it expressly for the great romantic actor, Frédérick Lemaître, whose passionate and disordered life matched that of the English actor who had recently died of his excesses.

Frédérick Lemaître had never entered the august ranks of the Théâtre Français where he was regarded with even greater horror than Marie Dorval. He had won his fame in the melodramas of the boulevards, as the wittiest, most cynical and most terrible of villains. He was hugely vain and could never see his name in large enough letters on the posters outside the theatre; when a manager asked where the names of his fellow actors could be printed he answered loftily: 'On the sticky side.' He had recently quarrelled with the Porte-Saint-Martin, where he had been the leading actor, and had found a refuge at the Théâtre des Variétés, till then the home of vaudeville and light comedy. It was here, on August 31st, after an unscheduled delay during which Dumas, who had neglected his duties as a member of the National Guard, served time in the Hôtel des Haricots as the prison for defaulters was known, that the first night of *Kean* took place.

Lemaître's performance was a *tour de force*. Never had his many-sided talents been displayed to better advantage. In the part of Kean, witty, drunken, passionate, as much at home in a fashionable salon as in a sailor's tavern, there was much of Dumas and much of Frédérick himself. In the cry of Kean on stage he summed up the whole romantic concept of dramatic art: 'I know that the life of orgies and debauchery I am leading is killing me . . . But what can I do? I am an actor. I must experience all life's passions in order to express them. I study them in myself to know them by heart.'

It was not a concept which could appeal to the classical school of acting, nor could they approve Frédérick's all too literal interpretation of his role: on several occasions, playing the drunken Kean, he came on drunk himself, once stopping to offer snuff to the prompter, another time launching into a tirade from a completely different play. *Kean* was an actor's triumph, received with enthusiasm by Frédérick's devotees. It could not win new converts to the romantic cause.

*   *   *

In June 1836, exasperated by her treatment at the Théâtre Français and harassed by debts which her salary there did not enable her to meet, Marie Dorval set off on a tour of the provinces where, if receipts were good, she could earn far more than in Paris. Her contract had allowed for an absence of three months. She would not return for nearly a year, driven from town to town and from one exhausting performance to the next by her desperate need to make money. Her greatest concern was her family. George Sand saw in her a *mater dolorosa*, perpetually at the mercy of her maternal feelings. It was this passion for her children that Vigny, saddened by his own childlessness, had depicted in the part of Kitty Bell. Marie Dorval's husband, Toussaint Merle, indolent and ailing, could no longer be relied on to support her daughters. Two of them, Louise and Caroline, were still at home; Louise, to her mother's despair, had followed the downward path of her sister and had taken a lover. Gabrielle, the eldest, had returned with Fontaney from England, where the hardships and privations she had encountered had fatally affected her health. She was dying slowly, though her mother at first had hopes she would recover, from tuberculosis. Fontaney, suffering from the same disease, was in little better shape. He was struggling bravely to keep her and himself on his meagre earnings as a journalist, and the two of them, defying public opinion (for he still refused to marry her) and her mother's pleas, had set up house together. Marie Dorval sent Gabrielle money secretly for fear of irritating Fontaney, relying on others to tell her her needs, for Gabrielle, clinging obstinately to her lover, left her letters unanswered.

Vigny came with Marie Dorval on the first stage of her journey to say goodbye. Not for them the carefree travels of Hugo and Juliette Drouet. To have accompanied her might have jeopardised her reputation in the eyes of respectable provincial audiences, for Marie Dorval's arrival in each new town was closely reported in the local press. 'You've often said to me,' she told him, consoling him for their separation, ' "Marie, I wish I were rich, I would give you all the money you need". *Eh bien*, you let me earn it, isn't that the same thing?'

They parted at Villeneuve-Saint-George, just outside Paris, and walked in the evening beside the river, Marie Dorval's head against Vigny's shoulder. From her carriage next day, laden with costumes for her coming tour, she wrote to him: 'I dreamt all night of the river's edge and our lumpy bed at Villeneuve-Saint-George. Never have you shown yourself more kind and tender. Always be my lover as you were yesterday and I can imagine no greater happiness in life. Try to find that little star by the river again, and call it Marie-Alfred. I swore before it to love you always and you made me the same vow . . . My little travelling carriage displeases me less now that you have visited it. I see the same countryside that we saw together, it gives an interest to everything around me. I am looking for a little *maison de berger* but I do not see one.'

The image of the *maison de berger*—the humble shelter which

shepherds wheeled behind their flocks—which they had seen together
remained in Vigny's mind, the germ of inspiration for his great philo-
sophical poem 'La Maison du Berger' eight years later. Was it the
memory of Marie Dorval that lingered in the final lines?

> Nous marcherons ainsi, ne laissant que notre ombre
> Sur cette terre ingrate où les morts ont passé;
> Nous nous parlerons d'eux à l'heure où tout est sombre,
> Où tu te plais à suivre un chemin effacé,
> A rêver, appuyée aux branches incertaines,
> Pleurant, comme Diane au bord de ses fontaines,
> Ton amour taciturne et toujours menacé.

Vigny returned to Paris, to days by his mother's bedside, 'turning
his spirit like a top' to amuse and distract her, and to his nights of
solitary study. He was planning a sequel to *Stello*—a sequel that would
never be completed. In July, leaving his mother in the care of two
maids, he set out to London with his wife on a visit to her family. There
were financial questions to be settled; Lydia's slender revenues were an
important part of their domestic economy. They spent two months
there passing the time agreeably enough in visits among the best
society. Vigny was a life-long anglophile. His English was fluent but
strongly accented: he had learnt it, he said, from Shakespeare and his
wife and the result was a quaint admixture of the archaic and the
domestic. He admired the gravity and calm of the English but felt that
they lacked the essential quality of the French, their gaiety of imagination. 'The supernatural efforts made by the French to establish a certain
warmth in their relations with English men and women', he wrote,
'will always be in vain: it is like drawing a violin bow across a stone.'
His strictures certainly included the fat and slumbrous Lydia.

For Marie Dorval, her apprehensions heightened by the fact that she
had received no letters from him for several weeks, even Lydia could
provide food for jealousy. 'My jealousy at knowing he is with her is
real,' she wrote to a friend, 'and I swear to you that he is obliged to
sleep with her. I am not in a state to mince my words, yes, sleep with
her, as they do in England. All the English sleep with their wives, they
won't have been given two rooms, he'll have wanted to show himself
a good husband to his father-in-law.'

Two letters from London put her out of her misery and she greeted
his return from England joyfully. 'O my angel, my Alfred, you're back,
you're back at last.' But she could not abandon her provincial journey-
ings yet; her travelling expenses had eaten up the profits she had hoped
for. 'I cannot come back to Paris until I have made money. I will not,

I cannot, suffer any more torments over money. I don't want it for myself but I must pay my debts, I must, I must.'

Marie Dorval's letters to Vigny continually protested her fidelity and her longing to be with him, but her vagabond life, when an evening's triumph would end with her return to a lonely hotel room, had included, she admitted to a woman friend, 'passing fancies of a month, a week, a day'. Vigny's jealousy, always on the alert, flared up, not at these unsuspected *passades* but at accounts of receptions and festivities held in her honour in the press. 'You cut me to the heart,' she wrote to him, 'in supposing that I lead a giddy and thoughtless life, when I have a daughter who is dying, whose groans I hear continually . . . You take the rouge which I put on my face for joy, and you believe me guilty of what others write about me.' And indeed the realities behind her successes on tour were harsh: exhaustion, squalid lodgings, rheumatism, colds and sickness are recurring themes in her letters. A letter to Vigny describes an evening when, after three days in bed, she acted in two successive pieces:

'I was hardly dressed when I was seized with the most violent stomach cramp I have ever had in my life. I played all my part in *La Muette* on the arm of one or other actor. But after this incredible effort I found myself in a state of such appalling weakness and spasms that it was only after an hour's interval that I was able to hold myself sufficiently upright to return on stage. In short, my angel, I played *Antony* leaving the scene each time to be sick and to vomit up all the ether and opium they had made me drink. Something extremely disagreeable and not at all pretty to describe even happened—I was in my ball gown and was taken with such violent stomach convulsions that no precautions could prevent all my tulle and satin dress and my poor white roses from being completely stained. Luckily for the last hour I had only drunk lemon and water, so it did not show too much, and I went on and played and the public applauded me more than ever, for they adore me in Avignon, and I was called back again and again.'

The hardships of Marie Dorval's travelling life, real though they were, may have had other compensations besides the money she needed so much, which was swallowed up as soon as she had earned it by creditors and her family. In Paris her daughter was dying. Her enemies at the Théâtre Français were doing all they could to prevent the renewal of her contract. Vigny's letters to her, though still assuring her of his love, were increasingly infrequent: she could sense his gradual withdrawal from her. Travel, activity, even exhaustion, provided an escape from facts which were too painful to face.

*   *   *

George Sand was passing through Lyon in October, after a summer spent travelling with Liszt and his mistress Marie d'Agoult. Marie Dorval, who was due to play there, wrote to reassure her lover. 'I will not see Madame Sand. But how am I to avoid her if she comes to see me? Tell me what I ought to do.'

Vigny's distrust of George Sand was still lively. 'O woman who makes yourself man,' he wrote, 'you are lost.' It was George Sand, he later told a friend, who had brought about Marie Dorval's ruin. The comment was enigmatic, reflecting more his own obsessions than the reality of their relationship. In Marie Dorval's last unhappy years when she would trail miserably from theatre to theatre, her looks and glory faded, George Sand would be a loyal and stalwart friend.

Meanwhile George Sand's husband, who was engaged in contesting her suit for a legal separation, was writing to his lawyer: 'There is one thing, I am told, which might make things difficult for Aurore in this case: she seems to believe that I have in my possession certain letters which it amused her to write to Madame Dorval, and which, from what I have heard and what I've discovered in Paris, are of a highly compromising nature. Could you not try to get hold of them through some sort of trickery? . . .'

The legal separation, however, was accomplished without recourse to the letters, and a satisfactory division of property, which had been her husband's chief concern, for George Sand's fortune exceeded his, was arranged between them. George Sand, who appeared in court looking modest and feminine in a simple white dress, was defended by Michel de Bourges, a young socialist lawyer who had become her lover six weeks after her final break with Musset. His star was already on the wane, however, and she was once more in pursuit of a new love, a young man to whom she carefully explained that her relationship with Michel de Bourges had been purely intellectual and that she had had no other lover since Alfred de Musset. As for Musset, she told him, she felt herself completely cured. She doubted if he ever thought of her except when he wanted to write a piece of poetry and earn a few sous from the *Revue des Deux Mondes*.

*   *   *

The memory of George Sand, the 'cruelle et froide amie', had indeed been revived in Musset's long poem 'Lettre à Lamartine' which was published in the *Revue des Deux Mondes* that spring. Addressing himself, not without diffidence—for Musset, unlike most of his romantic contemporaries, was essentially modest—to the famous poet of 'Le Lac', he recounted his own misfortunes in love which had left him, so he wrote, a living corpse from which the soul had fled.

Some years before, Sainte-Beuve had addressed Lamartine in a poem from *Les Consolations* and had been mortified by Lamartine's poem in reply, 'Epitre à Sainte-Beuve', which had mingled compliments with criticisms of his 'limping' verse and awkward style—a judgement which, wrote Sainte-Beuve in his *Cahiers*, had done more than any other to damage his reputation as a poet. Musset would fare little better. After reading his poem, Lamartine invited him to call and promised a poem in reply, an honour eagerly anticipated by the younger poet. The promised poem did not appear for nearly fourteen years and when it did, addressed Musset, by then nearly forty, as a fickle child:

Enfant aux blonds cheveux, jeune homme au coeur de cire.

'Lamartine vieilli qui me traite en enfant', wrote Musset in an angry sonnet.

Meanwhile, despite the despairing tone of the 'Lettre à Lamartine' Musset's life held many consolations. Social pleasures, expeditions with Alfred Tattet, evenings with the pallidly beautiful Princess Belgiojoso, of whom a contemporary once wrote, 'She must have been lovely when she was alive', were combined with a brilliant diversity of literary achievement, poetry, plays, literary and artistic criticism. In August appeared his 'Nuit d'août' in which he joyously proclaimed his return to the lists of love:

> J'aime et je veux chanter la joie et la paresse,
> Ma folle expérience et mes soucis d'un jour,
> Et je veux raconter et répéter sans cesse
> Qu'après avoir juré de vivre sans maîtresse,
> J'ai fait serment de vivre et de mourir d'amour.

He had already found new loves and new sources of suffering. There was Madame Jaubert, whom he christened his godmother and who called him Prince Café, because his company was a stimulant, and also, just as aptly, Prince Phosphore au Coeur Volant. Musset still fell in love as other people catch colds. There was a *grisette* who lived across the courtyard who became the model for his Mimi Pinson, and thus at one remove for the famous Mimi of *Scènes de la Vie de Bohème*. There was the fair-haired Aimée d'Alton who looked so fetching one evening in her white hooded cape that he sent her some verses the next morning, comparing her to a little white monk:

> Charmant petit moinillon blanc,
> Je suis un pauvre mendiant.
> Charmant petit moinillon rose,
> Je vous demande peu de chose,

Accordez-le-moi poliment,
Charmant petit moinillon blanc . . .

To the same Aimée d'Alton he recounted the lesson he had learned
from his experiences. 'To dream beautiful dreams and to wish to realise
them is the first essential in a noble heart. But once we are launched in
life reality, with its nauseating train, sooner or later attacks our young
virginal hope in its upward flight and strikes it down. This is no mere
apothegm, but an eternal truth. Aimée! The first experience consists in
suffering, it consists in discovering that absolute dreams are almost
never realised; or, if realised, that they wither and die when they come
into contact with the things of this world.' With George Sand he had
sought the absolute; from other women he would ask for less.

*   *   *

In May 1836 Hugo rented a small country house at Fourqueux, near
Saint-Germain, for his family. Here Adèle installed herself with her
father and her four children for the summer. Hugo left them in June to
travel in Brittany with Juliette Drouet, leaving his family with more
regret than heretofore. He wrote often and affectionately to his wife,
and Adèle, resigned and far from well, gave him her blessing:
'Never will I abuse the rights which marriage has given me over you.
In my mind you are as free as a young man, my poor friend, who married at only twenty. I do not wish you to tie your life to a poor woman
like me. At least what you give me will be given freely, and without
compulsion. So do not torment yourself and believe me when I say that
nothing in my own state of mind will alter my tender feelings for you,
which are so firmly based and so devoted despite everything.'
Such indulgence carried more weight than reproaches. 'I do not want
you to be sad, my Adèle,' wrote Hugo anxiously, 'I cannot be happy if
you are unhappy. If these journeys make you sad I will not go any more.
After all, and before all, you are still my beloved Adèle.'
Juliette Drouet rightly saw in Hugo's solicitude for his wife a reflection on herself. She felt that his love for her, once all-absorbing, was
tainted with pity and a sense of duty. She complained of prolonged
periods of chastity—it is possible that Hugo, whose love affairs would
be without number, was already not entirely faithful, and that the
private staircase which led to his room in the Place Royale had been
used by others than herself. Even their travels together that summer
were spoiled for her by the presence of an unwelcome third, Célestin
Nanteuil, a young artist whom Hugo had invited to accompany them
to record the sights and monuments they visited, and with whom he
vied good-naturedly in sketching them.

[119]

But Juliette's place in Hugo's life, though from now on in the wings, was fixed. Two years later he would take upon himself a solemn engagement, regarded by her like a secret vow of marriage, never to abandon her or her daughters. She had won him, said Frédérick Lemaître, by saying 'You are great,' she would hold him by saying 'You are beautiful'. Her adoration, her daily love letters to him, 'like so many mirrors', he told her, 'each one reflecting another aspect of your lovely spirit', were a necessity to him. Despite storms and scenes their relationship held firm, Hugo working to the point of exhaustion to support his two households, Juliette accepting the life of poverty and sequestration which he imposed on her with almost mystical self-abnegation. Gone were the lavish silks and laces which had framed her beauty as a courtesan; she was reduced to two or three dresses, much mended and made over. Eggs, cheese and apples were her staple diet, except when Hugo came to supper, when she would prepare a delicious meal, such as he seldom had at home. Adèle, with all her virtues as a mother, was an appalling housekeeper.

Hugo returned to Paris at the end of July to attend rehearsals of an opera *Esmeralda*, based on his *Notre-Dame de Paris*, with music by Louise Bertin, daughter of Louis Bertin with whose family he had stayed at Bièvre in previous summers. He went back and forth to Fourqueux, never staying long, bringing a gust of vitality into the peaceful routine of a life whose greatest event was otherwise a visit from the curé. Fontaney, whom he invited to spend a night there, described him presiding at dinner 'without a jacket, in his shirt, that is to say in his wife's peignoir, superb in his gaiety'. When Fontaney returned to Paris the following afternoon he found that poor Gabrielle, whom he had left behind, had been striking the bust of Hugo, which he, like all good romantics, had on display in his room, in her impatience at the length of his absence.

In September, Léopoldine, aged twelve, made her first communion in the parish church of Fourqueux and was painted for the occasion, looking composed and serious, by Auguste de Châtillon. Her mother, who had a charming talent for painting, had done other portraits of her that year; indeed all that summer, according to Adèle's father, she had been buried in her drawing, refusing distractions and amusements.

Away from Paris, her religious sentiments perhaps revived by the preparations for her daughter's first communion, Adèle Hugo showed herself increasingly reluctant in her love for Sainte-Beuve. Her health was not good, she seemed to be passing through some crisis of depression. 'If I write to you rarely,' she told Sainte-Beuve, 'it is because I have no joy to bring you, no certain hope to offer; my heart is broken and withered; it is only when it overflows with bitterness that it forces me to write to you. My friend, never think me dead towards you; there is still enough in my affection to make you happy, believe me. It is an affection that kills many others more lively and more immediate. Keep your heart for me, I count on it with certainty; the tie between us is fortified by time and seeming calm. It is a tenderness that grows in silence. Oh! believe this, my poor friend.'

When she returned to Paris, after a five-months' absence, their reunion brought no lift of spirits. Without drama, without painful scenes, Sainte-Beuve could feel her slipping away. 'Another thought continues to give me pain,' he wrote to her; 'it is the feeling that some change is taking place in you—some kind of struggle, as though you were sacrificing hopes and illusions which had become too dear to you . . . Adèle, I have always been poorly endowed with the faculty of hope; I have always felt some hindrance or deficiency in everything; my sentiments have always lacked the sun, even in the height of summer . . . As for a happiness crowned with pleasure I have always had little faith in that for us. I have renounced it in my heart far more definitely than I seemed to have on those too frequent occasions when my desires importuned you. If you were more devout and you wished to transport our love entirely to the realms of religion I would never importune you so and our sad happiness would be unalloyed. But there, I love you from the depths of my soul and I know that it is the same with you; is that not a sublime consolation? Let us then be neither gay nor joyful, but let us not be unhappy.'

But even at this unambitious level the 'sad happiness' he hoped for eluded him. Adèle Hugo had come to terms with her husband's infidelity and in doing so, perhaps, had grown to value more what was left to her: her position as the wife of a great man and as the mother of his children. Both she and they depended entirely on Hugo's literary earnings. Whatever her personal reservations, the maintenance of Hugo's fame and reputation was of direct concern to her. In placing himself in the ranks of Hugo's enemies Sainte-Beuve threatened her also. His open hostility to her husband could only work against him in her eyes.

In a short novel, *Madame de Pontivy*, written that autumn, Sainte-Beuve found other reasons for the decline of their love. The heroine, Madame de Pontivy, is a portrait of Adèle, the hero, Monsieur de Murçay, of Sainte-Beuve. Their love for one another, in the absence of her husband, is ruined by the hero's lack of ardour; the exclusiveness of Madame de Pontivy's passion is not matched by that of her lover. Out of pride, and in an effort to dampen the heat of her own emotions, she withdraws herself more and more from him and it is only too late that he realises that the love on which he had counted is dying from sheer lassitude.

In the book there is an explanation and a reconciliation, and the lovers come together once more in a steadier and more balanced relationship. In real life there would not be any happy ending; and the turn of the year brought forth from Sainte-Beuve the despairing poem whose last line he would repeat in his novel:

Laissez-moi! Dans nos champs, les roches solitaires,
Les bois épais appellent mon ennui.
Je veux, au bord des lacs, méditer leurs mystères,
Et comment tout m'a fui . . .

Laissez-moi! Midi règne et le soleil sans voiles
Fait un désert à mon oeil ébloui.
Laissez-moi! C'est le soir, et l'heure des étoiles;
Qu'espérer? Tout a fui.

Oh! laissez-moi, sans trêve, écouter ma blessure,
Aimer mon mal et ne vouloir que lui.
Celle en qui je croyais, celle qui m'était sûre . . .
Laissez-moi, tout a fui.

11

1837

Ten years had passed since Hugo's first meeting with Sainte-Beuve, the founding of the Cénacle, the challenge to classical tradition flung down in the preface to *Cromwell*. Hugo and Sainte-Beuve were now unshakeable enemies. The Cénacle was dissolved and its members had gone their different ways. The great era of romantic drama which the preface to *Cromwell* had heralded was coming to an end.

For Dumas, whose *Henri III et sa Cour* had opened the way at the Théâtre Français, 1837 was the year of his decisive defeat in the same arena. His career as a dramatist was not yet over: his natural joviality, long concealed by the bloodshed and violence of romantic drama, would sparkle forth in a series of delectable comedies; his career as a novelist, as the creator of Monte Cristo and the three musketeers, had not yet begun. Nonetheless, 1837 marked an ending and a turning point for him, though typically the collapse of his play *Caligula* was a comic not a tragic episode.

Dumas had been inspired originally, it was said, by reports of a performing horse, whom he hoped to cast in the role of the horse Incitatus, created consul by Caligula. The performing horse had died while he was still studying Suetonius but, determined not to waste his work, he had continued with the play and presented it on completion to be read at the Théâtre Français. The subject, drawn from Roman history, was the most classical he had yet undertaken. The play was accepted with enthusiasm by the committee, his first to be considered there since the banning of *Antony* three years before.

Thanks to Dumas' influence his mistress, Ida Ferrier, had obtained a place at the Théâtre Français and it was to her that the part of the heroine, a Christian virgin abandoned to the lubricity of Caesar, was entrusted. The production was mounted at immense expense but the management drew the line at Dumas' request, in the absence of the performing horse, for four other horses to draw Caesar's chariot across the stage. He was forced to content himself instead with arranging for medallions, engraved on one side with the head of Caligula and on the other with the date of the first night, to be sold in the foyer—a desecration of the theatre which shocked more sober spirits.

But neither medallions nor the lavish stage effects could save the play. Dumas' intention, unkind friends remarked, had been to inspire pity for the inadequacy of Racine's *Britannicus*. The naivety and pretension of his attempt were greeted with derision. Ida Ferrier, monstrously fat in her Roman robes, tripped over her draperies; the critics called her the 'callipygian martyr'. The leading actor, who did not appreciate his role, dismissed an annoying colleague with the phrase, *Tu me caligulades*, and the expression was repeated joyously by others.

Dumas wasted little time in licking his wounds. Together with Victor Hugo he was planning to start a new theatre, devoted to the works of the romantic school, with the encouragement of the Duc d'Orléans, eldest son of Louis-Philippe, whose interest in the romantics had already been demonstrated by his support of *Chatterton*. But the great days of romantic drama were nearly over. Hugo's masterpiece, *Ruy Blas*, in 1838, was the last real success in the genre and in 1843, when his next play, *Les Burgraves*, failed disastrously, he abandoned the stage for ever.

*   *   *

In October 1837 Alfred de Musset wrote the last and perhaps the most perfect of his 'Nuits', 'La Nuit d'octobre'. The dialogue between the poet and his muse starts quietly:

Le mal dont j'ai souffert s'est enfui comme un rêve;

then, as memory revives, the poet's slumbering resentment rises to a crescendo:

Honte à toi qui la première
M'a appris le trahison,
Et d'horreur et de colère
M'as fait perdre la raison!
Honte à toi, femme à l'oeil sombre,
Dont les funestes amours
Ont enseveli dans l'ombre
Mon printemps et mes beaux jours! . . .

It was the last spasm of the passion that had changed him, he said, from a child to a man.

Sainte-Beuve, who had followed the drama of Venice and its aftermath so closely and given counsel on both sides, had now fallen out with George Sand. He had had enough, he said, of her 'sublime scribblings'. She in her turn had lost patience with him. 'I loved him like a brother,' she wrote to Liszt. 'He passed his time in vexing me, in scolding me, in suspecting me to such an extent that I ended up by sending him to the devil.'

But Sainte-Beuve remained on friendly terms with Musset, finding him 'extremely amiable and nice, though perhaps at heart so spoilt and ruined'. In earlier days—for a taste for venal pleasures was the counterpart of Sainte-Beuve's romantic love for Adèle—they had visited a brothel together. Now, in a poem from *Pensées d'Août*, a collection published that autumn, he compared their unhappy experiences of love: his own, which had declined after seven years into silence, Musset's, which had drained him of his youth and joy,

Comme un fruit qu'on méprise après l'avoir séché . . .

His private opinion of George Sand he confided to his notebook: 'For a long time I was close to the woman who wrote *Lélia*, like a man at the brink of an abyss whose edges are covered with lush and smiling vegetation, and reclining in the high grass I was filled with admiration. But one day, in the end, I leant over and I saw: *O quanta Charybdis.*'

Sainte-Beuve's *Pensées d'Août* were his farewell to poetry. His future as the greatest critic of the nineteenth century lay before him. The laborious edifice of the *Causeries de Lundi* would be built up step by step; he had already begun work on his history of Port-Royal, begun while he was still searching for some glimmering of religious belief, completed more than twenty years later when faith was dead. Meanwhile, in a phrase in an article that year, he had written his own poetic epitaph: 'There exists in most men a poet who died young, whom the man survives.'

His present position was melancholy. The stream of poetic inspiration, of which he had hoped so much in the first days of his friendship with Hugo, seemed dried up; the hostile reception given by critics to his *Pensées d'Août* confirmed him in his loss of confidence. Though his authority as a critic had never been greater, he was poorly paid, and he felt himself insufficiently honoured by those in power. In June 1837, on the occasion of the marriage of the king's son, the Duc d'Orléans, he touchily refused the offer of the ribbon of the Légion d'Honneur, feeling cheapened by being included in a list of writers inferior to himself.

Above all his love for Adèle, or rather hers for him, seemed to be dying from its own inanition. Their meetings, like their letters, had grown fewer and fewer. 'The health of Madame H. worries me greatly,' he wrote to his friend Guttinger. 'She had an accident this autumn at Fourqueux. Since then irregularities and illness. The trouble has redoubled in these last months. She keeps to her room, is unable to go out, either on foot or in a carriage. I get direct news of her only with great difficulty and at very long intervals. Alas! The other evening, under a radiant sky, I pushed my way through the happy crowds, howling and sobbing like a wounded stag.'

In October he left Paris to take up an appointment at the University of Lausanne where he was to deliver a series of lectures on the history of Port-Royal. '*She* has abandoned me', he wrote to Victor Pavie while waiting to hear that his appointment was confirmed, 'and I consider myself now free to leave and go into exile. She is, besides, sad and unwell; her life is becoming more and more colourless without her being aware of it, or seeking any remedy or distraction.'

He did not leave without a final scene. That March his novel *Madame de Pontivy* had been published in the *Revue des Deux Mondes*. His admitted intention had been to appeal to Adèle and to draw her back, as in the book, into a harmonious relationship. His appeal found no response from Adèle; the novel, with its transparent allusions to a love that had been gratified, could only infuriate Hugo. It was this perhaps which was the subject of the confrontation to which Sainte-Beuve referred in a letter to Guttinger the following summer:

'When I left Paris in October my mood was gloomy, trebly gloomy . . . So far as Place Royale is concerned I had had an experience which only a brief talk between us could make clear: on one side a coarse and murky bit of scheming in which I could smell the Cyclops,* on the other an unbelievable and truly stupid credulity which gave me the measure of an intelligence no longer enlightened by love . . .'

His love for Adèle Hugo had been the one great passion of his life. 'I have only had one great and true success in love (my Adèle)', he wrote in a private note, 'and since then have been like those generals who live on one great victory . . . From then on I have always been defeated, one failure following another. I have grown weary of doing battle, I no longer enter into it and content myself humbly with a few minor manoeuvres in the countryside. But what do I care anyway? I have found my Adèle and her heart and no longer wish to love any but her.'

The note is dated 1840. It is followed by a later entry: 'Illusion! I have lost her again and I hate her; she no longer has a heart, she never had any intelligence.'

*   *   *

On the occasion of the wedding of the Duc d'Orléans, Hugo, already a chevalier of the Légion d'Honneur, had been invited to a banquet and reception at Versailles, and was about to accept when Dumas called on him, in great indignation, complaining that his name had been struck off the list of wedding honours by Louis-Philippe and that he had in consequence sent back his invitation. Hugo generously

* A term Sainte-Beuve often used in speaking of Victor Hugo. He described his *Ruy Blas* in the following year as 'an omelette mixed by Polyphemus'.

sent his own refusal to the Duc d'Orléans, explaining his reasons for doing so. The Duke, an admirer of both writers, persuaded his father to put Dumas' name back on the list and the two friends, now reconciled, set off to the reception together. The Princesse d'Orléans, a widely read and romantically-minded young German princess, made a special point of meeting Hugo: she had read all his poems, she told him, and had visited 'his' Notre-Dame. A few weeks later, on the publication of his new collection of poems, *Les Voix Intérieures*, she and her husband sent him a handsome painting as a token of their admiration. From then on they multiplied their attentions to him, inviting him not only to formal receptions but to the intimate evening gatherings they held once a week. The king himself, adding to the favours offered by his son, promoted Hugo to the rank of officer of the Légion d'Honneur.

Hugo's ambitions were moving from the purely literary to the political. As a poet and a dramatist he had seen himself as an interpreter of society to itself: a 'sonorous echo' set in its midst. His sympathy for the poor and the oppressed and his passionate opposition to the death penalty had been consistently expressed in his work. Now he sought a public platform. He lacked the property qualifications to be a deputy; his only other route to political power lay through the Chamber of Peers. To be named as a peer Hugo must first be a member of the Academy. He had already, in the previous year, stood unsuccessfully as a candidate but had received sufficient votes to encourage him in further attempts. The support of the Duc d'Orléans, whose liberal opinions were close to Hugo's, would be an important element in ensuring his acceptance.

In March 1837 Hugo's elder brother, Eugène died, after fourteen woeful years of confinement in a madhouse. His reason had first succumbed on the night of Hugo's marriage. In his early youth he had shown a talent almost as great as Hugo's; they had entered literary life side by side. His fate had always been the sombre reverse of Hugo's glory. Hugo mourned the loss of the companion of his childhood and the destiny which had cast him into darkness, leaving Hugo to the hatreds and conflicts of the market-place:

> Quel choc d'ambitions luttant le long des routes,
> Toutes contre chacune et chacune avec toutes!
> Quel tumulte ennemi!
> Comme on raille d'en bas tout astre qui décline . . .
> Oh! ne regrette rien sur la haute colline
> Où tu t'es endormi! . . .

Despite his worldly successes that year Hugo had never felt himself more surrounded by enemies. The defection of Sainte-Beuve, above all, in whom it has been suggested he had sought a compensation for the fraternal relationship broken by his brother's madness, was a continuing source of bitterness. 'It was an envious man I had taken for a friend,' he wrote later. 'He had the hostility which derives from former intimacy and thus is armed from top to toe.' The publication of *Madame de Pontivy* in March must have been the occasion for a string of savage verses against the 'viper', never published in his lifetime, for Hugo preserved an imperturbable dignity towards the outside world, but confided at least to Juliette. 'I have copied out your splendid verses on the treachery of a false former friend,' she wrote to him. 'They are as sublime and agonising as the conflict of the eagle and the viper.'

Hugo left with Juliette Drouet that summer on the yearly holiday that was her compensation for the loneliness of her life in Paris. Indefatigable sightseers, they travelled rapidly through Normandy and Belgium, leaving not a church or a ruin unexplored. Adèle Hugo complained that her husband's letters to her, which ran to many pages, were devoted entirely to descriptions of the sights he had seen; could he not, she asked him, give a little space to personal messages for her and the children? Less complaisant than in previous years—for Sainte-Beuve was no longer in her life—she insisted that her husband should not prolong his absence beyond a month, and that next year it should be she who should accompany him on his travels. 'I am, I think, within my rights in saying this,' she wrote.

Hugo, his first triumphant years with Juliette over, was experiencing the strains as well as the pleasures of a divided love: on the one hand the complaints of Juliette, too often, she felt, set aside in favour of Hugo's social life, on the other the claims of Adèle, whose indifferent health was a further cause for worry. Only his children remained an unalloyed delight. 'Toute ma poésie,' he wrote, 'c'est vous.'

In October, leaving Juliette behind, Hugo returned to Metz and the valley of Bièvre where in earlier years he and Juliette had met and loved in secret. He spent five days there, revisiting the woods, the garden, the isolated house where she had stayed, scenes of their happiness together. From the visit was born his great poem 'Tristesse d'Olympio' in which, taking on himself the person of Olympio, his poetic alter-ego, he reflected with melancholy on the flight of time and nature's indifference in the face of memory. In evoking the first days of his passion for Juliette he also, by implication, announced their decline:

> Pâle, il marchait.—Au bruit de son pas grave et sombre
> Il voyait à chaque arbre, hélas! se dresser l'ombre
> Des jours qui ne sont plus! . . .

For Juliette the poem which more than any other immortalised their love marked the ending of its first and happiest chapter. Hugo wrote of memories, Juliette, her thoughts still in the present, longed only to revive them with a return to the beloved valley which her lover, preferring his thoughts to her company, had visited alone. 'I'd so much like to make an excursion there,' she wrote wistfully. 'Your beautiful verses have made me want to even more . . . Today would have been such a good day for an expedition. It's beautifully warm and sunny. What a pity you don't feel like it . . .'

*   *   *

Vigny's love for Marie Dorval was foundering. What years of scenes and jealousy had failed to accomplish in Paris Marie Dorval's year-long absence would achieve. 'All my life was spent by your side,' he wrote in his journal when everything was over. 'I struggled against everything that surrounded you and was hostile to me. I overcame the frightful disgust which your home and those who lived there inspired in me. All to see you and to live in your presence.

'Presence, presence! Divine source of comfort! Necessity which sustains love with the constant contemplation of the loved one. Presence which brings unfailing reassurance—against death, in which one no longer believes when faced with so much life; against forgetfulness, which eyes and words deny; against infidelity itself, which no longer seems possible.

'This need you did not understand, you took it for an insignificant impulse of jealousy.

'One can love too much. I would not have believed it.'

The death throes of their love were long-drawn-out. It was not until 1838, when both had openly betrayed the other, Marie Dorval with Jules Sandeau, George Sand's first lover, Vigny with two young English girls, Julia and Maria Battlegang, that Vigny would write in his journal the inexorable word *RUPTURE* and both would go their separate ways, Marie Dorval on a downward course of poverty, ill health and failure, Vigny to his 'ivory tower',* to live more and more removed from the hurly-burly of the literary battles in which his robuster companions delighted.

Marie Dorval died ten years later, in abject misery. Dumas and Hugo raised the money for her funeral expenses. A year later there was a new production of Vigny's play *Quitte pour la Peur*, with a much praised young actress, Rose Chéri, in the leading part. 'I am perhaps the only

* . . . Vigny, plus secret,
   Comme en sa tour d'ivoire, avant midi, rentrait . . . (Sainte-Beuve).

person in Paris who has not seen it,' wrote Vigny to a cousin. 'And if I ever saw it—ought I to say this? Yes, why not?—it would rend my heart, for it would seem to me, in thinking of the woman for whom it was written, that they had parted her garments among them and cast lots upon her vesture.'

For the new year, 1837, Marie Dorval sent Vigny a parcel of gifts. She enclosed money for her daughters, sixty francs to buy a green silk wrapper for Gabrielle, who, ill though she was, still had moments of coquetry and gaiety.

Marie relied on Vigny to visit her family and give her news of them. But his letters had grown rarer. It seemed to her, she wrote in February, that he had abandoned her home. What could her husband have said to him that had not made him pity her rather than be angry? His long silences were killing her. Did he think she was happy? Her successes brought her no joy. She could never be happy or vain of her triumphs with the constant awareness of his sadness and their separation, and the phantom of her daughter always in her thoughts.

On the 15th of April Gabrielle died, at the age of twenty-one. Marie Dorval's husband deliberately hid the news from her, but a letter from Vigny gave her the presentiment of some disaster. She compared the two letters and was reassured by that of Merle. 'Your letter, which I received yesterday,' she wrote to Vigny, 'caused me an uneasiness which I am unable to express. It seemed as though you were addressing a cry to me, sending an impulse of your soul towards me to console me —for what new sorrows? "Marie, Marie, you do not have me to weep with you" . . . I did not dare continue. I opened the letter of M. Merle which arrived with yours, I was trembling violently but from the first line I felt reassured and the tone of his letter throughout did not permit me to believe that some calamity had occurred in Paris. I returned to your letter, dear love, and once again was overcome . . . But the letter of M. Merle says nothing, nothing. I must have been mistaken.'

It was not till she returned to Paris in June that she received the news of her daughter's death. Overcome with grief, she spoke for a time of abandoning the stage, of entering a convent. But before long a renewed engagement at the Théâtre Français and the prospect of another provincial tour plunged her once more into activity and the partial oblivion of the theatre's unreal emotions.

*   *   *

'My poor martyr died this morning at eleven o'clock,' wrote Fontaney to Sainte-Beuve on the day of Gabrielle's death. 'The funeral will take place at Saint-Sulpice at eleven tomorrow.' Fontaney himself had only two months to live. His last work, written in a struggle against increasing weakness, was a novel recounting the story of his love for Gabrielle, piteous in its remorse for not having given her the consolation of marriage and in its painful certainty of his own impending death.

Gabrielle was buried in the cemetery of Montparnasse. With pride Fontaney noted that he had been able to pay for a decent burial. 'Everything had been arranged at the town hall. There was a covered hearse, a grave set apart for five years, an engraved headstone with a cross above, a wooden balustrade in black oak, two little cypresses at the right and left of the grave, the grass sown with violets and daisies thinly scattered around.'

Hugo and Sainte-Beuve had attended the funeral service. They entered the church of Saint-Sulpice by different doors. It was the end of mass, the crowd was streaming out, the final blessing was about to be pronounced. Hugo came in on the Gospel side, Sainte-Beuve hid himself in the opposite aisle. 'But hatred, like love,' wrote a witness to the scene, 'has a sixth sense; they did not see one another, but they felt each other's presence.'

After the funeral service, by a singular coincidence, the two found themselves forced to take the same carriage to the cemetery. They sat face to face, their knees touching. Hugo, calm and impassive, talked to the unfortunate Fontaney. Sainte-Beuve, in agony, said not a word and stared fixedly out of the window. 'If he could have flown away,' recalled a fellow passenger, 'he would certainly have done so; each step of the journey was torture to him. They remained like this for half an hour.'

'What a funeral,' wrote Sainte-Beuve to Ulric Guttinger a few days later. 'And in the cemetery of Montparnasse as well, near places once so filled with happiness for us . . . And in our hearts a friendship that was dead, more dead than her we buried.'

Appendix: Translations

EIGHTEEN TWENTY-SEVEN

p6   My soul has its secret, my heart has its mystery.

p7   On Sundays, gay as the bird on the branch, we sometimes kept the Arsenal awake till morning . . .

Someone recited something, in verse or prose, then we rushed to begin dancing again . . .

So, in that great romantic bazaar, everyone, master or boy, had his own song . . .

Hugo already carried Notre-Dame in his soul and was beginning to scale it. De Vigny sang on his lyre of that fine gentleman who died without turning his green stockings back to front . . .

Sainte-Beuve, in the soft and sombre shadows, wrote a sonnet to a dark eye, a white cap.

And I, all unworthy of this signal honour, a spoilt child adopted by chance, I embroidered ballads, one to the moon, the other to two black and jealous Andalusian eyes . . .

p9   No brothers! no, Frenchmen of this expectant age! We have all grown up on the threshold of the soldier's tent. Condemned to peace, young eagles banished from the skies, let us at least, jealous sentinels, guarding our fathers' glories, protect the arms of our ancestors from all insult!

EIGHTEEN TWENTY-EIGHT

p18   Your genius is great, my friend, your thoughts mount like Elisha in the living chariot of Elijah . . .

EIGHTEEN TWENTY-NINE

p27   A genius has risen up amongst you in the thick of the storm, young and strong, indignation imprinted on his brow in lightning flashes; but here he lays down his sceptre and discards it, his glory without its brilliant rays grows kind and gentle and greets all eyes with laughter.

Oh, long may he sing! for his lute leads us on, rallies us and guides us, and for as long as it resounds we shall hold the field. Two or three times round again and to the sound of his trumpet and the thunder of his voice, which a whole choir re-echoes, Jericho will fall.

p31   Await me, woman, I come! Your blood, soon to be shed by my propitiated hand, will flow on the bed which your offence has sullied.

p33   You are my lion! superb and generous!

p33   Alas, I love nonetheless with the profoundest love. Do not weep, let us rather die. Had I the world I would give it to you. I am truly unhappy.

p34   Where (when the cat roams and howls in the mist) Monsieur Hugo goes to watch fair Phoebus die.

p34   It was murky night, the moon on the yellowing steeple like the dot on an *i*.

EIGHTEEN THIRTY

p39   Can it be he already? Someone indeed is at the hidden staircase.

p42   Beloved beings, pure objects of my immortal admiration. Oh, if my destiny carried me far away and you forgot me, or if, still near you, you almost ceased to think of me, here, far away and forever, you will still be all in all to me. Happy and brilliant pair, I only live in you.

p43   Friends, my two friends, my painter, my poet! I miss you all the time and my disquieted soul longs for your presence here.

p48   I would have gone out then but you said to me 'Stay!' and raining through your fingers your heavy tresses gave forth the scents of seed-time.

EIGHTEEN THIRTY-ONE

p54   A beauty, always in tears, passing amidst other figures, like a pale ray of light through sombre forests, simple, sad and terrible.

p57   Woe, woe to me, whom Heaven has cast into this world, a stranger alien to its laws. To me, who knows not, in my bitter anguish, how to suffer long without revenge.

p61   Adèle! tender lamb! What struggles take place in the shadows when your jealous lion returns, beside himself, sombre-voiced, usurping his place by your side, demanding his rights, his share in your beauty, and you, broken, fainting, gripped in his arms of steel, will always find some unbelievable ruse to keep yourself faithful to your timid conqueror who does not wish for, and will never have, more than your heart.

EIGHTEEN THIRTY-TWO

p63   I do not wish to dwell in the city of the living save in a house which the sound of children fills with life and fantasy.

p69   Oh! the incense of the theatre is an impure incense. Above, the brilliant actor, below the obscure crowd, one amid lights, the other in the dust, begin their vulgar struggle in the night.

p69   We must hold a book open on our knees and follow it with our eyes; we must speak and laugh, or I must be heard reading, and when my voice expires you tremble for us both.

Your door is just ajar and its rose-coloured curtain is so thin that one can overhear everything, a chair move, a sigh, a pause; and I am the stranger;

And I am the *visitor*, and if, in the eternal chit-chat my voice is heard to hesitate, if, through my imprudence, someone suspicious detects my silence, he will say: 'What is he doing?'

Since we are surrounded by others I will go on speaking in a monotone, I will appear to continue reading, but I escape from them and it is another book which I will unfold:

It is my heart, it is my soul, it is love for a woman in a man of fire; desire, delirium, agitation, weariness, rage, hope, in the end . . . madness which should be locked away . . .

Do you feel the earth move? Your room shake? Do you not see the sky shadow over? Day flees before nature. Where is your sash? Go on, continue reading. Night falls on my eyes.

Ah! your very hair is trembling and despite yourself mingles with the hair on my brow. Ah! your cheek is burning beneath my trembling lips. Ah! how swiftly my slow fever catches fire.

They are there, listening to me, suspecting, doubting, they are there, they are all there. But all constraint is vain, your heart bears the imprint of mine, and despite our fears I have told you all this.

EIGHTEEN THIRTY-THREE

P77 Your imprisonment is at last alleviated, for he, hard and jealous, arrogant and injured, has been caught in the trap of an insane love. Night and day he pursues the object which draws him on, and we, quick to profit from each short respite, fly no less swiftly to the nearest woods . . .

P78 Before long, each withdrawing to a hideous realm, Woman will inhabit Gomorrah and Man Sodom, and casting from afar an angry glance at one another, the two sexes will die, each on its own side.

p84 Sand, when you wrote of it, where had you witnessed that terrible scene where Noun, half naked, swoons in the arms of Raimond on the bed of Indiana?

p85 George is in her little room, between two pots of flowers, smoking a cigarette, tears streaming from her eyes.

Buloz, seated on the ground, makes soft protestations to her; Solange, behind, scribbles on her novels.

Stuck like a milestone, Boucoiran, soaking wet, contemplates the dishevelled Musset with a mournful eye.

Planche, drunk since last night, is seated in a corner, picking his ear with the greatest care.

p86 I do not believe, O Christ, in your holy word: I have come too late into a world that is too old . . . Your glory is dead, O Christ, and on our ebony crosses your heavenly corpse has turned to dust. So be it! May we at least, credulous children of this century without faith, kiss the dust and weep, O Christ, on this cold earth, to which your death gave life, and which will die without you. Oh! who now, my God, will give it life once more? With your purest blood you had restored its youth. Jesus, who is there now, to do what you once did? Old men, born yesterday, who will restore our youth?

p86 We carry in our hearts the rotting corpse of the faith by which our fathers lived.

EIGHTEEN THIRTY-FOUR

p96 Oh! if somewhere beneath the heavens you meet a woman whose brow is pure, whose step is measured, whose eyes are gentle, and whom four children follow, the last one tottering . . . Oh! whoever you may be, give her your blessing. It is she, the sister of my immortal soul, before my eyes. It is she, my pride, my hope, my shelter, my resource, home of my youthful years and hope of my old age.

p96 It was a humble church we entered, with a low arched roof, where for more than three hundred years full many a soul had made their way and wept.

It was sad and calm at the close of day, the church we entered; the untended altar, like a heart without love, was without its flame.

p97 Oh, Madame, why this grief which follows you? Why do you still weep, woman whose heart is so enchanting, dark as the night, soft as the dawn? What does it matter that life, unequal here below for man and woman, seems to flee and break before you? Have you not still your soul?

Your soul, soon perhaps to fly elsewhere, to purer realms, carried far away, beyond our sorrows, beyond our sighs.

Be, then, like the bird, poised for an instant on a bough too frail for it, who feels the branch bending and yet still sings, knowing that it has wings!

EIGHTEEN THIRTY-FIVE

p103 When you have proved, gentlemen of the press, that Chatterton did wrong to die unknown, that he has been misrepresented at the Théâtre Français, when you have cried out seven times against atheism, seven times against absurdity and seven times against sophism you will not have proved that I did not weep.

p104 Poet, take up your lute and give me a kiss. The briar rose feels its buds begin to bloom. Spring is born tonight; the winds grow warm, and the wagtail, awaiting the dawn, alights on the first green bushes. Poet, take up your lute and give me your kiss.

How black the valley seems! I thought a veiled form floated yonder in the forest. She came out from the meadow, her foot just touched the flowering grass. It is a strange reverie; it dissolves and vanishes.

p104 Nothing makes us greater than a great sorrow ... The most despairing songs are the most beautiful, and I know immortal ones which are pure sobs.

p105 When I die, dear friends, plant a weeping willow by my grave.

p110 When I am no more than coldest ashes, when my tired eyes are closed to the day, say to yourself, if my memory is still fixed in your heart: 'The world had his thoughts, *I* had his love.'

EIGHTEEN THIRTY-SIX

p115 Thus we shall walk, leaving only our shadows on this ungrateful earth where the dead have passed before. We shall speak of them at that darkling hour when you loved to follow some forgotten path and to dream, leaning against the tremulous branches, weeping like Diana beside her fountains for your silent and always threatened love.

p118 Child with the golden hair, young man with heart of wax ...

p118 Lamartine grown old, who treats me as a child.

p118 I love; and I wish to sing of joy and idleness, my mad experience and my fleeting sorrows, and I wish to affirm and repeat without cease that after having sworn to live without a mistress I have made a vow to live and die for love.

p118 Charming little white monk, I am a poor suppliant. Charming little rose-pink monk, I am only asking very little, please grant it me politely, charming little white monk.

p122 Leave me! in our fields the solitary rocks and darkening woods call forth my melancholy. By the shores of lakes I wish to meditate upon their mysteries and think how all has fled.

Leave me! Midday reigns and the unveiled sun creates a desert for my dazzled eyes. Leave me! It is evening and the hour of stars. What hope is there? All has fled.

Oh! Leave me without respite to feel my wound, to love my pain and wish
for nothing else. She in whom I trusted, she who seemed so sure . . . leave me,
all has fled.

EIGHTEEN THIRTY-SEVEN

p124 The pain which I suffered has fled like a dream.

p124 Shame on you who first taught me treachery and drove me to madness from
horror and rage. Shame on you, woman with sombre eyes, whose fatal loves
have buried my spring-time and my young days in shadows.

p125 Like a fruit which is scorned, having been drained dry.

p127 What clash of ambitions battling along the way, one against the other and
each against all, what tumult of the enemy! How men mock the star which
declines . . . Oh! regret nothing on that high hill where you now sleep.

p128 *You* are all my poetry.

p128 Pale, he walked on; to the sound of his grave and melancholy footsteps he
saw by each tree, alas, rise up the shadow of days which are no more.

p129 Vigny, more discreet, retired to his ivory tower before midday.

Bibliography

Apart from the works mentioned in the text the following are among the books consulted. English books are published in London, French books in Paris, unless otherwise stated.

Allem, Maurice: *A la gloire de . . . Musset* (Nouvelle Revue Critique, 1940)
Allem, Maurice: *Portrait de Sainte-Beuve* (Albin Michel, 1954)
Audiat, Pierre: *Ainsi vécut Victor Hugo* (Hachette, 1947)
Baldick, Robert: *The Life and Times of Frédérick Lemaître* (Hamish Hamilton, 1959)
Barbier, Auguste: *Souvenirs Personnels et silhouettes contemporaines* (Dentin, 1883)
Benoît-Lévy, E.: *Sainte-Beuve et Madame Victor Hugo* (La Renaissance du Livre, 1927)
Berlioz, Hector: *Mémoires* (Michel Lévy, 1870)
Berlioz, Hector: *Memoirs*, translated by David Cairns (Victor Gollancz, 1969)
Billy, André: *Sainte-Beuve, sa vie et son temps* (Flammarion, 1952)
Bray, René: *Chronologie du Romantisme. 1804–1830* (Boivin, 1932)
Carr, Philip: *Days with the French Romantics* (Methuen, 1932)
Castelnau, Jacques: *Adèle Hugo* (Jules Tallandier, 1941)
Clouard, Henri: *Alexandre Dumas* (Albin Michel, 1955)
Conference du Musée Carnavallet (1930): *La Vie Parisienne à l'époque romantique* (Payot, 1931)
Davidson, A. F.: *Victor Hugo, his life and work* (Eveleigh Nash, 1912)
De la Salle, Bertrand: *Alfred de Vigny* (Fayard, 1962)
De Berthier de Sauvigny, G.: *La Révolution de 1830 en France* (Armand Colin, 1970)
Descotes, Maurice: *Le Drame Romantique et ses grands créateurs* (Presses Universitaires, 1955)
Dorval, Marie: *Lettres à Alfred de Vigny*, receuillies et présentées par Charles Gaudier (Gallimard, 1942)
Draper, F. W. M.: *The rise and fall of French romantic drama* (Constable, 1923)
Drouet, Juliette: *Mille et une lettres d'amour à Victor Hugo*. Choix, préface et notes par Paul Souchon (Gallimard, 1951)
Du Camp, Maxime: *Souvenirs Littéraires* (Hachette, 1882)
Dumas *fils*, Alexandre: *Affaire Clémenceau* (Michel Lévy, 1869)
Dumas *père*, Alexandre: *Mes Mémoires* (Michel Lévy, 1863)
Dumas *père*, Alexandre: *Souvenirs dramatiques* (Michel Lévy, 1868)
Dupuy, Ernest: *Alfred de Vigny* (Société Française d'Imprimerie et de Librairie, 1910)
Escholier, Raymond: *Un Amant de Génie: Victor Hugo* (Arthème Fayard, 1953)
Fontaney, Antoine: *Journal Intime*, publié avec une introduction et notes par René Jasinski (Presses Françaises, 1925)
Gautier, Théophile: *Histoire du Romantisme* (Charpentier, 1874)
Gribble, Francis: *The Passions of the French Romantics* (Chapman & Hall, 1910)
Guillemin, Henri: *Victor Hugo par lui-même* (Editions du Seuil, Collection 'Ecrivains de Toujours', 1951)
Haldane, Charlotte: *Alfred: the Passionate Life of Alfred de Musset* (Anthony Blond, 1960)
Henriot, Emile: *L'Enfant du Siècle: Alfred de Musset* (Amiot Dumont, 1953)
Houssaye, Arsène: *Les Confessions* (Dentu, 1885)
Houssaye, Arsène: *Souvenirs de Jeunesse: 1830–1850* (Flammarion, 1896)

Hugo, Adèle: *Victor Hugo raconté par un témoin de sa vie* (Brussels, Lacroix, 1863)
Hugo, Victor: *Correspondance* (Calman-Lévy, 1896)
Hugo, Victor: *Choses Vues, 1830–1846*. Edition établie, présentée et annotée par Hubert Juin (Gallimard, 1972)
Hugo, Victor: *Lettres à Juliette Drouet*. Texte établi et présenté par Jean Gaudon (Jean-Jacques Prévert, 1964)
Lamartine, Alphonse de: *Portraits et Salons Romantiques*. Introduction de Louis Barthou (Le Goupy, 1927)
Lanson, Gustave: *Histoire de la Littérature Française* (Hachette, 1952)
Lauvrière, Emile: *Alfred de Vigny, sa vie et son oeuvre* (Grasset, 1945)
Lehman, A. G.: *Sainte-Beuve: a portrait of the critic, 1804–1842* (Oxford University Press, 1962)
Maigron, Louis: *Le Romantisme et les Moeurs* (Librairie Ancienne, 1910)
Maurois, André: *Lélia: La vie de George Sand* (Hachette, 1952)
Maurois, André: *Olympio: la vie de Victor Hugo* (Hachette, 1954)
Maurois, André: *Les Trois Dumas* (Hachette, 1957)
Maurois, André: *Lélia*, translated by Gerard Hopkins (Jonathan Cape, 1953)
Mérimée, Prosper: *Correspondance Générale*. Etablie et annotée par Maurice Parturier (Le Divan, 1941)
Moreau, Pierre: *Le Romantisme* (Del Duca, 1957)
Musset, Alfred de: *Correspondance (1827–1857)*, receuillie et annotée par Léon Séché (Mercure de France, 1907)
Musset, Alfred de: *Lettres d'amour à Aimée d'Alton*. Introduction et notes par Léon Séché (Mercure de France, 1910)
Musset, Paul de: *Biographie d'Alfred de Musset* (Charpentier, 1877)
Musset, Paul de: *Lui et Elle* (Charpentier, 1877)
Nicolson, Harold: *Sainte-Beuve* (Constable, 1957)
Olivier, Juste: *Paris en 1830*. Publié par André Delattre et Marc Denkinger. Préface de Fernand Baldensperger (Mercure de France, 1951)
Raitt, A. W.: *Life and Letters in France: the nineteenth century* (Nelson's University Paperbacks, 1970)
Sainte-Beuve, Charles-Augustin: *Les Cahiers* (Alphonse Lemerre, 1876)
Sainte-Beuve, Charles-Augustin: *Souvenirs et Indiscretions* (Michel Lévy, 1872)
Sainte-Beuve, Charles-Augustin: *Mes Poisons*, publiés avec une introduction et des notes par Victor Giraud. (Plon, 1926)
Sand, George: *Correspondance*. Textes réunis, classés et annotés par Georges Lubin (Garnier Frères, 1966)
Sand, George: *Elle et Lui* (Calman-Lévy, 1889)
Sand, George: *Correspondance inédite avec Marie Dorval*, publiée avec une introduction et des notes par Simone André-Maurois (Gallimard, 1953)
Sand, George: *Correspondance avec Alfred de Musset*, texte établi, annoté et présenté par Louis Evrard (Monaco, Editions du Rocher, 1956)
Saunders, Edith: *The Prodigal Father* (Longmans, Green & Co., 1951)
Séché, Léon: *Alfred de Musset* (Mercure de France, 1907)
Séché, Léon: *Le Cénacle de Joseph Delorme* (Mercure de France, 1912)
Sedgwick, Henry Dwight: *Alfred de Musset* (Indianapolis, Bobbs Merrill Company, 1931)
Starkie, Enid: *Petrus Borel* (Faber, 1954)
Thackeray, W. M.: *The Paris Sketch Book* (Harper, 1911)
Tieghem, Philippe van: *Dictionnaire de Victor Hugo* (Larousse, 1970)
Toesca, Maurice: *Alfred de Musset ou l'amour de la mort* (Hachette, 1970)
Toesca, Maurice: *Vigny ou la passion de l'honneur* (Hachette, 1972)

BIBLIOGRAPHY

Viallenex, Paul: *Alfred de Vigny par lui-même* (Editions du Seuil, Collection 'Ecrivains de Toujours', 1964)

Vigny, Alfred de: *Correspondance, 1816–1835*, notes et éclaircissements de Fernand Baldensperger (Louis Conrad, 1933)

Whitridge, Arnold: *Alfred de Vigny* (Oxford University Press, 1933)

Index

A quoi rêvent les jeunes filles (Musset), 83
Affaire Clémenceau (Dumas *fils*), 83
Agoult, Marie d', 117
Alton, Aimée d', 118, 119
Amy Robsart (Hugo), 19, 26
André (Sand), 91
Andrea del Sarto (Musset), 86
Angelo, Tyran de Padoue, 107, 109
Antony (Dumas), 55, 56, 65, 93, 94, 103, 116, 123
Arvers, Félix d', 6

Balzac, Honoré de, 4, 28, 38, 71, 101
Barbier, Auguste, 30
Barrault, Jean-Louis, 86
Battelgang, Julia, 129
Battelgang, Maria, 129
Baudelaire, Charles, 103
Belgiojoso, Princess, 118
Berlioz, Hector, 4, 12, 13, 20, 45
Berry, Duchess de, 66, 74
Bertin, Louis-François, 73, 96, 120
Bertin, Louise, 120
Billy, André, 110
Bocage, Pierre, 56, 81
Borgia, Lucrezia, 75
Boucoiran, Jules, 85
Boulanger, Louis, 4, 28, 42
Bourges, Michel de, 117
Buloz, François, 67, 85, 91, 103
Bunbury, Hugh, 15
Burgraves, Les (Hugo), 124
Byron, George Gordon, Lord, 4, 32, 87

Caligula (Dumas), 123
Caprices de Marianne, Les (Musset), 86
Causeries de Lundi (Sainte-Beuve), 125
Chandelier, Le (Musset), 105
Chants du Crépuscule, Les (Hugo), 110, 111
Charles X, 8, 9, 25, 26, 29 36, 43–46, 66
Charles VII et ses Grands Vassaux (Dumas), 65
Chateaubriand, François-René, Vicomte de, 5, 8, 9, 14, 59, 71
Châtillon, Auguste de, 120

Chatterton (Vigny), vii, 94, 101–103, 106–109, 124
Chatterton, Thomas, vii, 67, 101–103
Chénier, André, 67
Chéri, Rose, 129
Christina, Queen of Sweden, 21
Christine (Dumas), 21, 22, 40, 41
Cinq-Mars (Vigny), 14, 68, 106
Claude Gueux (Hugo), 107
Confession d'un Enfant du Siècle, La (Musset) 91, 105
Consolations, Les (Sainte-Beuve), 47, 118
Constitutionnel, Le, 93
Contes d'Espagne et d'Italie (Musset), 34, 51, 52
Corneille, Pierre, 10, 14, 20, 58, 112
Coupe et les Lèvres, La (Musset), 83
Cromwell (Hugo), 11, 13, 14, 19, 20, 123
Cromwell, Oliver, 10

David d'Angers, 4, 25, 28
Deburau, Jean Gaspard, 86
Delacroix, Eugène, 4, 11, 12, 19, 26, 28, 51, 74, 98
Delavigne, Casimir, 112
Demidoff, Anatole, 75, 81, 96, 97
Dernier Jour d'un Condamné, Le (Hugo), 26
Deschamps, Antony, 4, 28, 51
Deschamps, Emile, 4, 14, 19, 20, 28
Devéria, Achille, 4, 28, 35, 51
Devéria, Eugène, 4, 26, 28, 34, 35
Don Juan da Marana (Dumas), 112
Dorval, Caroline, 114
Dorval, Gabrielle, 92, 93, 114, 120, 130, 131
Dorval, Louise, 114
Dorval, Marie, 10, 16, 53–56, 58, 59, 64, 68–72, 78, 79, 92–94, 100–102, 106–109, 112–117, 129, 130
Drouet, Juliette, 75, 76, 79–82, 95–97, 109–111, 114, 119, 120, 128, 129
Du Camp, Maxime, 102
Dudevant, Maurice, 85, 88
Dudevant, Solange, 72, 85, 88
Dumas, Alexandre, *père*, 4–6, 16, 18, 20–26, 28, 29, 31–33, 40, 41, 45, 51, 52, 54–57, 62, 64–66, 71, 76, 78, 81–83, 93, 101, 112, 113, 123, 124, 129

Dumas, Alexandre, *fils*, 24, 57, 58, 82, 83

Elle et Lui (Sand), 85, 87
Eloa (Vigny), 30
Enfants du Paradis, Les, 86
Esmeralda (Hugo), 120

Ferrier, Ida, 82, 112, 123, 124
Feuilles d'Automne, Les (Hugo), 59, 60, 63, 111
Fieschi, Guiseppe, 105
Firmin, François Becquerelle, 33, 55
Flaubert, Gustave, 76, 103
Fontaney, Antoine, 59, 60, 63, 64, 74, 92, 93, 114, 120, 130, 131
Foucher, Paul, 18–20
François I, 73

Gaillardet, Frédéric, 64, 65
Gautier, Théophile, 4, 13, 41, 51, 56, 58, 73, 101–103
Génie du Christianisme, Le (Chateaubriand), 9
George, Mlle (Marguerite-Josephine Weymer), 11, 40, 53, 58, 64, 65, 75, 76, 81, 82
Gilbert, Nicolas, 67
Globe, Le, 1, 3, 9, 17, 28, 30, 39, 46, 47
Goethe, Johann Wolfgang, 4
Guêpes, Les 47
Guise, Duc de, 23, 25
Guizot, François, 27
Guttinger, Ulric, 42, 43, 125, 126, 131
Hamlet (Shakespeare), 11
Han d'Islande (Hugo), 1
Harel, Charles-Jean, 40, 58, 64, 65, 75, 112
Henri III, 22, 25
Henri III et sa Cour (Dumas), 23–26, 29, 32, 41, 123
Hernani (Hugo), 10, 30, 32, 36, 37, 39–42, 46, 56, 58, 65, 68, 94, 107, 108
Houssaye, Arsène, 15, 47, 50, 72
Hugo, Adèle, *née* Foucher, 2, 5, 14, 15, 17, 27, 36–39, 41, 42, 46–49, 59, 61, 64, 72, 73, 76, 77, 79, 80, 83, 95–97, 107, 108, 110, 111, 119–121, 125, 126, 128
Hugo, Charles, 5, 63, 64
Hugo, Eugène, 127

Hugo, François-Victor, 17
Hugo, Léopold, 5
Hugo, Léopoldine, 5, 50, 73, 110, 120
Hugo, Victor, 1–11, 13–20, 25–43, 46–50, 52, 58–61, 63–65, 68, 73–77, 79–82, 86, 93–97, 101, 107–112, 114, 119–121, 123–129, 131

Illustrated London News, The, 12
Indiana (Sand), 71, 77, 84
Jacques (Sand), 91
James II, 36
Jaubert, Caroline, 118
Journal des Débats, Le, 73, 81

Karr, Alphonse, 50
Kean ou Désordre et Génie (Dumas), 113
Kemble, Charles, 11, 12
Krelshamer, Belle, 57, 82

Lafayette, Marie-Joseph, Marquis de, 45
Lamarque, General Maximilien, 66
Lamartine, Alphonse de, 3, 4, 6, 8, 9, 15, 18, 59, 117, 118
Latouche, Henri de, 32
Lebay, Catherine, 24, 57
Lélia (Sand), 77
Lemaître, Frédérick, 10, 53, 54, 75, 76, 113, 120
Lerminier, Jean-Louis, 86
Leroux, Pierre, 45
Liszt, Franz, 4, 63, 98, 100, 117, 124
Livre d'Amour, Le (Sainte-Beuve), 47, 72
Lorenzaccio (Musset), 89, 91
Louis XIII, 29
Louis XVI, 43, 44
Louis XVIII, 8
Louis-Philippe (Duc d'Orléans, afterwards Roi des Français), 20, 24, 25, 44, 45, 62, 66, 67, 74, 94, 124, 126
Lucrèce Borgia (Hugo), 75, 76, 81
Borgia, Lucrezia, 75
Luguet, René, 82

Madame de Pontivy (Sainte-Beuve), 121, 126, 128
Magnin, Charles, 39
Maigron, Louis, 57
Malibran, Maria-Garcia, 25
Maréchale d'Ancre, La (Vigny), 53, 68
Marie Tudor (Hugo), 81, 96, 109

INDEX

Marion de Lorme (Hugo), 28–30, 58–60, 68
Marmont, Duc de Raguse, 44
Mars, Mlle (Anne Boutet), 12, 20, 29, 32, 33, 38–40, 53, 55, 58, 94, 107–109
Medici, Catherine de, 23
Méditations, Les, Lamartine, 18
Merle, Jean-Toussaint, 53, 69, 114, 130
Mérimée, Prosper, 4, 5, 51, 63, 78, 83
Mirabeau, Victor Riqueti, Marquis de, 94
Misérables, Les (Hugo), 107
Molière (Jean-Baptiste Poquelin), 20
Moore, Thomas, 32
Musset, Alfred de, 4–7, 18–20, 28, 34, 51, 52, 62, 63, 68, 78, 83–92, 98–100, 103–105, 117, 118, 124, 125
Musset, Paul de, 87

Nanteuil, Célestin, 119
Napoleon I, Emperor, 8, 9, 11, 20, 37, 40, 64, 74
National, Le, 36
Nerval, Gérard de, 4, 11, 51
Nodier, Charles, 5–8, 18, 19, 21, 22, 29, 32, 34, 40, 51, 54, 66
Nodier, Mme, 6
Nodier, Marie, 6
Notre-Dame de Paris (Hugo), 46, 50, 59, 60, 68, 107, 120
Nuit Vénitienne, La (Musset), 52

Odes et Ballades (Hugo), 1, 3, 18
On ne badine pas avec l'amour (Musset), 91
Orientales, Les (Hugo), 20, 26, 28, 51
Orléans, Duc d', 94, 124–127
Orléans, Duc d' (Philippe Egalité), 44
Orléans, Princesse d', 127
Othello (Vigny's translation), 20, 28, 30–32, 52, 68

Pagello, Pietro, 90–92, 98–100
Pailleterie, Marquis de la, 20
Paris Sketch Book (Thackeray), 112
Pavie, Victor, 18, 26, 73, 76, 110, 126
Penseés d'Août (Sainte-Beuve), 125
Piccini, Alexandre, 53, 69
Planche, Gustave, 67, 85, 87, 109
Polignac, Prince Jules de, 29, 36, 43, 44
Pradier, Charles, 75

Quenouille de Barberine, La (Musset), 105

Quitte pour la Peur (Vigny), 79, 129
Quotidienne, La, 32

Rachel, Mlle (Elisa Félix), 112
Racine, Jean, 10, 20, 26, 112
Racine et Shakespeare (Stendhal), 11
Récamier, Juliette, 5
Revue des Deux Mondes, La, 50, 67, 68, 83, 85, 86, 91, 103, 111, 117, 126
Richard Darlington (Dumas), 82
Richelieu, Armand Jean du Plessis de, Cardinal, 14, 106
Rigoletto (Verdi), 73
Robespierre, Maximilien François de, 67
Roi s'amuse, Le (Hugo), 68, 73–76
Romantisme et Les Moeurs, Le (Maigron), 57
Romeo and Juliet (Shakespeare), 12, 19
Roméo et Juliette (Deschamps and Vigny), 19, 20, 22, 30
Rose et Blanche (Sand and Sandeau), 71
Ruy Blas (Hugo), 124

Sainte-Beuve, Charles-Augustin, 1–5, 7, 9, 12, 15–20, 26–28, 31, 32, 34–37, 39, 40, 42, 43, 46–50, 59–61, 68, 71–74, 77–81, 83, 89, 92, 94–96, 98–100, 103, 110, 111, 118, 120–126, 128–131
Sand, George (Aurore Dudevant), 53, 71, 77–79, 83–92, 98–101, 109, 114, 117, 119, 124, 125
Sandeau, Jules, 71, 77, 87, 129
Saint-Just, Antoine de, 67
Scenes de la Vie de Bohème (Murger), 118
Scott, Sir Walter, 4, 6, 9
Shakespeare, William, 4, 11, 12, 21, 28, 30, 31, 87, 112
Siddons, Sarah, 12
Smithson, Harriet, 11, 12
Spectacle dans un Fauteuil, Un (Musset), 83, 86
Stello (Vigny), 67, 101, 106, 115
Stendhal (Henri Beyle), 5, 8, 11, 40, 88
Sully, Maximilien de Béthune, Duc de, 6
Swinburne, Algernon Charles, 89

Tableau Historique et Critique de la Poésie Française au XVIe Siècle (Sainte-Beuve), 17

Talleyrand-Périgord, Charles-Maurice de, Prince of Benevento, 44
Talma, François-Joseph, 10, 11
Tattet, Alfred, 98, 100, 104, 118
Taylor, Baron Isidore-Justin-Séverin, 19–23, 29
Thackeray, William Makepeace, 112
Thiers, Adolphe, 44
Tour de Nesle, La (Dumas), 64–66
Trente Ans dans la Vie d'un Joueur (Gobaux, Beudin, Ducange), 10, 53
Trois Mousquetaires, Les (Dumas), 14
Turquety, Edouard, 28

Valentine (Sand), 77
Vampire, Le (Nodier), 21, 22

Verdi, Guiseppe, 73
Vie, Poésie et Pensées de Joseph Delorme (Sainte-Beuve), 26, 42
Vigny, Alfred de, vii, 4–9, 12, 14–16, 18–20, 25, 26, 28–32, 35, 39–41, 45, 46, 50, 52–54, 62, 67–69, 71, 72, 78, 79, 92–94, 101, 103, 105–107, 109, 112, 114–117, 129, 130
Vigny, Lydia de, née Bunbury, 14, 15, 93, 115
Voix Intérieures, Les (Hugo), 127
Volupté (Sainte-Beuve), 79

Waldor, Mélanie, 57
Wellington, Arthur Wellesley, Duke of, 11, 36